# ASTON MARTIN

## THE DB LABEL

From the DB2 to the DBX

Serge Bellu

Preface by Marek Reichman

# ASTON MARTIN

## THE DB LABEL

From the DB2 to the DBX

images
Publishing

First published in France in 2021 by Editions Glénat
© Editions Glénat 2021 – ALL RIGHTS RESERVED
24 Avenue du Maréchal de Lattre de Tassigny CS 80269
92772 BOULOGNE-BILLANCOURT CEDEX
France
www.glenat.com

Published in Australia in 2022 by
The Images Publishing Group Pty Ltd
ABN 89 059 734 431

Offices

*Melbourne*
Waterman Business Centre
Suite 64, Level 2 UL40
1341 Dandenong Road
Chadstone, VIC 3148
Australia
Tel: +61 3 8564 8122

*New York*
6 West 18th Street 4B
New York City, NY 10011
United States
Tel: +1 212 645 1111

*Shanghai*
6F, Building C, 838 Guangji Road
Hongkou District, Shanghai 200434
China
Tel: +86 021 31260822

books@imagespublishing.com
www.imagespublishing.com

Copyright © The Images Publishing Group Pty Ltd 2022 (English Edition)
The Images Publishing Group Reference Number: 1664

English translation by David Watson

A catalogue record for this book is available from the National Library of Australia

Title:    Aston Martin: The DB Label, From the DB2 to the DBX
Author:  Serge Bellu
ISBN:    9781864709469

This title was commissioned in IMAGES' Melbourne office and produced as follows:
*Editorial* Georgia (Gina) Tsarouhas, Jeanette Wall *Graphic design* Ryan Marshall *Production* Nicole Boehringer

Printed by Graphius nv, Belgium, on 150gsm Magno Matt art paper

IMAGES has included on its website a page for special notices in relation to this and its other publications.
Please visit www.imagespublishing.com

# CONTENTS

# PREFACE

At Aston Martin, design is everything. Serge Bellu has been a fan of the brand for years, and his book masterfully explores the significance of design for Aston Martin through the work of the designers who created its finest and most memorable models.

He is one of the very few people I would trust to evoke the long and winding road that is the history of design at Aston Martin.

Serge Bellu's experience of our cars goes all the way back to the launch of the Aston Martin Lagonda, designed by William Towns. Since then, he has driven almost every model that our firm has produced. So his book draws on a vast knowledge of the company. As you read these pages, you will see the evolution of Aston Martin from the founding of the company in 1913 to the David Brown era and beyond. You will come to understand the way in which the aesthetic standards of the past still influence the designs of today, in spirit if not in the actual forms.

It needed the experienced eye of an outside observer to bring these legends back to life. Serge Bellu has written about, taught and assessed the art of bodywork for many years; so his mastery of the subject and his affinity for the creativity of car design are second to none. Over the course of nine chapters, he tells the story of Aston Martin in terms of the great stylistic periods that have marked out its history. In doing so, he picks out the formal and technological innovations which still echo down to today.

Establishing how beauty and modernity are to be defined in the Aston Martins of tomorrow for me is a privilege, but also a responsibility. For a designer, an understanding of history is just as important as an aptitude for design. I know that all my colleagues in the Aston Martin design studio share my passion for, and my interest in, the countless fascinating stories that have punctuated this great British make of ours.

It is a great honor for me to be among the list of designers who have taken part in this adventure. Reviewing all the successes of my predecessors, I realise that Aston Martins are much more than merely the cars that we draw out in our studios and build by hand in our factories in Gaydon and St Athan. They form part of a rich heritage. Each modern Aston Martin bears a sense of history and, more importantly, has the duty to express a timeless beauty.

Marek Reichman,
Chief Creative Officer, Aston Martin,
Gaydon, UK, March 2021

Marek Reichman, Chief Creative Officer and Executive Vice President of Aston Martin Lagonda.

# THE DB LABEL

The initials 'DB' are now better known than the person they are derived from. David Brown crossed paths with Aston Martin for only twenty-five of the hundred-plus years of the company's history, between the years of 1947 and 1972. But it was during those crucial years, thanks to the decisive drive of David Brown, that the Aston Martin brand was transformed. Under his guidance, it went from being a modest artisanal workshop producing bespoke sports cars to one of the world's most prestigious car manufacturers.

Long after the departure of their instigator, the initials DB are today still bestowed on the company's most ambitious models: DB11, DBS Superleggera, DBX. All these jewels are the latest in a long and magnificent line stretching back to the original DB2, which came out in 1949.

It is the story of these DBs that I will be telling here, with passing references to the other models that were developed alongside them.

As well as David Brown and his successors, I wanted to pay homage to the backroom boys, the artists who gave form to Aston Martin's cars. It is the stylists and designers who have driven the changes in the firm and preserved its unique character. Thanks to them, this singular brand is still distinguished by its restraint, by the elegance of its designs, by the discretion of its styles, by a reserve that is all too rare in a world more often noted for its exuberance.

Thanks to the input of all its creators, Aston Martin has managed to survive both the internal crises and the economic shocks that have peppered its history.

A new chapter covers Aston Martin's return to Formula 1 in 2021. I now invite you to discover the stages of this history of a great British ambition.

Serge Bellu

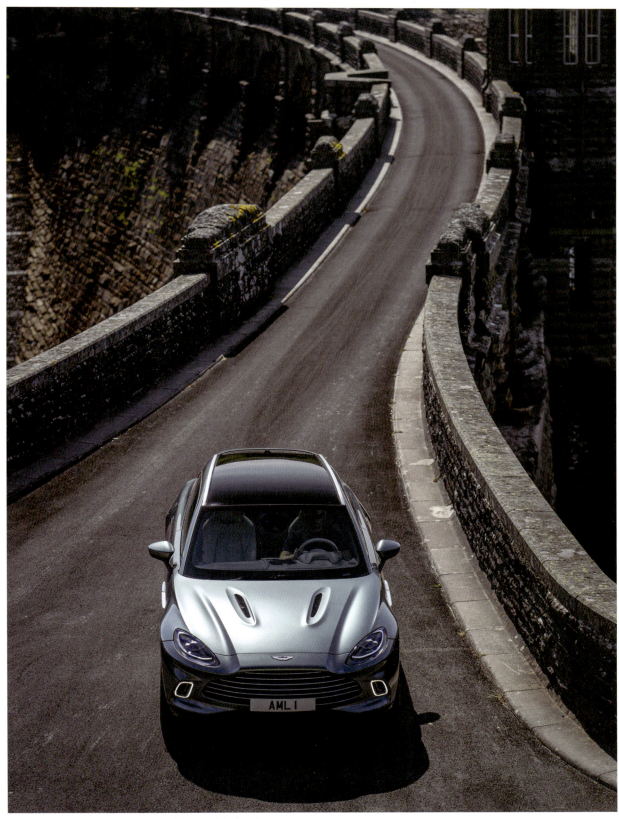

The DBX marks a new adventure in the saga of the 'DBs'.

Lionel Martin lent his name to a legend in the history of the car.

# ASTON MARTIN BEFORE DAVID BROWN (1913–1947)

An unbelieving world was going about its business unaware that, just a year later, one of the bloodiest conflicts in history was about to break out. In Paris, opinion was divided over a new ballet. The premiere of *Rite of Spring* on 20 May 1913 at the Théâtre des Champs-Élysées had offended conservative sensibilities. On the other side of the Atlantic, in a different context, Henry Ford was also overturning convention and triggering a new industrial revolution. On 1 December, the Model T Ford began rolling off the production line in a factory in Highland Park.

When the firm of Bamford & Martin was founded in 1913, no one had an inkling that the name of a small town in Buckinghamshire would come to replace the surname of the co-founder of the enterprise on the eve of the First World War. David Brown was then just nine years old and could scarcely imagine that one day he would help this paternal company flourish and indeed lend his initials to one of the most beautiful dynasties in the history of the car. It is in the years between 1913 and 1947 that the brand was formed, that it grew, established its notoriety, defined its personality and established the first landmarks of its rich history, albeit one with many ups and downs. In this introductory chapter we evoke those early flashes of brilliance.

At the opposite pole of this frenetic mass production and standardisation there were a number of craftsmen who were modest in their ambitions and carefree in their passions. Among them were Robert Bamford (aged thirty) and Lionel Martin (aged thirty-five), partners in a small garage on the outskirts of London. These two motor enthusiasts adapted their business model and began selling cars made by Singer: on 15 January 1913 they established Bamford & Martin Ltd, which was based at 16 Henniker Place in South Kensington. In their workshop on the periphery of the commercial centre, they indulged their love of sport by adapting the small Singer Ten for racing. Bamford drove the car to great success, notably in a hard-fought hill climb at Aston Clinton, a charming little village in Buckinghamshire, which would soon lend its name to the two men's products.

The first model produced by the Bamford & Martin workshop in 1913, known as the 'Coal Scuttle' because of the rounded shape of its bodywork.

The good results they achieved using the Singer encouraged the pair to go further and construct their own prototype. They put together a roadster using an old Isotta Fraschini chassis, to which they added a 1.4-litre Coventry Simplex engine. They completed the car in March 1915 and nicknamed it the 'Coal Scuttle' because of its shape. The firm's work was disrupted by the First World War, but once peace was declared their activity began to take off in earnest.

Robert Bamford retired in 1920, and Lionel Martin was left in sole charge of the business and able to devote himself to a project that was close to his heart: to produce cars to his own design. To enable this, he moved to new premises in Abingdon Road, West Kensington, and employed the engineer H. A. Robb to help him create his first pre-series models. The gentleman driver and wealthy patron Count Louis Zborowski came on board around the same time, injecting some cash subsidies into the business and providing a steering hand alongside Lionel Martin. He commissioned the French engineer Marcel Grémillon, who had formerly worked for Peugeot, to create a new engine. Zborowski financed the construction of several racing cars, notably the car nicknamed 'Bunny', which clocked up speed records at Brooklands in May 1922, and the two machines that contested the Grand Prix de l'Automobile Club de France in July. The cars were known as the 'Green Pea': they were fond of nicknames at Aston Martin.

Between 1922 and 1925, the workshop in West Kensington produced over sixty cars. Seven of these were racing cars. This wasn't enough. The financial situation worsened, and to add further misery Count Zborowski was killed at the wheel of a Mercedes at the Italian Grand Prix in 1924.

Back to square one. The company, now ruined, passed into the hands of the Charnwood family, under the direction of Lady Charnwood and her son, the future Lord Charnwood. Production was halted for several months and the company was placed into liquidation. The firm was relaunched under the name Aston Martin Motors Ltd, registered in October 1926. Lord Charnwood turned for help to two engineers, William Somerville Renwick and Augustus Cesare Bertelli. The company moved to a new factory on Victoria Road, Feltham, to the west of London.

**Top:** An 11 HP in a hill climb in the early 1920s. **Above:** A 1½-litre Ulster private (BS/549/U) at Targa Abruzzo in August 1935.

Bertelli's input would prove to be decisive for the brand. He developed a commercial range based on the 1½-litre model powered by a brand new four-cylinder overhead camshaft. Launched at the London Motor Show in 1927, the 1½ litre would undergo three phases of development:

• Series 1 (October 1927), with either short wheelbase (S-Type) or long wheelbase (T-Type); the International version appeared in October 1929. 136 were produced, of which fourteen were T-Type.

• Series 2 (February 1932), characterised by a new chassis and a Laycock transmission; this line included T-Type, International and Le Mans versions, 130 were produced.

• Series 3 (1934 onwards), which corresponded to the arrival of the Mark II, available as a 2-/4-seater roadster, convertible (DHC), a 4-seater Torpedo tourer and a sports saloon. The peak of the range was the brilliant Ulster. 166 were produced, including sixty-one roadsters, forty-five tourers, twenty-four sports saloons, twenty-one Ulsters and seven drophead coupés.

Alongside this output, Aston Martin produced machines especially for racing (numbered LM1 to LM21), which distinguished themselves at the Le Mans 24 Hours between 1928 and 1935. They won their class several times, and in 1935 an Ulster finished third overall. Most of the 1½ litres had their chassis applied in the bodywork workshop of Enrico Bertelli—the brother of Augustus Cesar—a neighbour of the Aston Martin factory in Feltham.

The firm continued to encounter financial difficulties and had to be rescued more than once, first by Lance Prideaux-Brune and then by Sir Arthur Sutherland.

The 2-litre Speed Model during the Le Mans 24 Hours in 1938. It did not finish the race.

**Top left:** A singular 1½-litre Mark II (no. K4/513L) saloon. **Top right:** A simple chassis produced at Aston Martin cladding the last 2 litres to go under the name of C-Type. **Above:** One of the 2-litre 15/98s (no. G0/871/SO) with convertible chassis by Abbey Coachworks in 1939.

In 1936, the 1½ litre was replaced by the Speed Model, a sporty roadster with cycle wings (a type of mudguards) equipped with a new 2-litre engine developed by Claude Hill, originally intended to race at the Le Mans 24 Hours which was cancelled due to a strike. To make some profit from their investment, they developed a more touristy version of the original. This 2-litre 15/98 unveiled at the London Motor Show in 1936 was offered in the form of a saloon manufactured by E. Bertelli Ltd (about fifty) or a convertible produced by Abbey Coachworks (about twenty) out of a total of 176. In 1937, A. C. Bertelli left the firm over a dispute with the son of the owner, which brought an end to the collaboration between his brother Enrico and Aston Martin.

The last eight chassis, which proved difficult to dispose of, were produced at the factory under the reference Type C in a more enveloping style.

Feltham ground to a halt. Fresh blood was needed.

David Brown, the entrepreneur who bought Aston Martin in 1947.

# DB2: THE ORIGINS OF THE MYTH

The DB1 never existed, at least not under that name. The Aston Martin lineage bearing the initials 'DB' only really began with the DB2.

In June 1947, an inconspicuous small ad appeared in *The Times*. The Aston Martin Ltd company was up for sale at a price of £20,500. One savvy reader spotted it. His name was David Brown. Born on 10 May 1904, he was the director of a solid family business founded by a grandfather who had the same name as him. The company originally manufactured wooden gears for looms, but when the sons of David Brown Snr, Frank and Percy, took over the business in 1903, they developed complete drive components. The third generation took up the reins in 1931 on the death of Percy Brown, and his son David became the managing director of the firm.

At the Le Mans 24 Hours in 1939, Lagonda entered a superb model with a somewhat anachronistic style, driven by the 12-cylinder engine conceived by W. O. Bentley.

# THE COMING OF DAVID BROWN

As soon as he took charge of the family business, David Brown decided to expand its field of activity into agricultural machinery. To expedite matters, he first of all considered a partnership with Harry Ferguson, but in the end the latter turned to Henry Ford. David Brown set off on his adventure alone and produced his first tractors in 1939.

After the end of the war, Brown was more than ever on the lookout for new opportunities. Why not the car industry, which needed to rebuild itself after six years of conflict? He signed the cheque to acquire Aston Martin the following year and he bought Lagonda, a less artisanal manufacturer, for £52,500. The fates of these two brands, Aston Martin and Lagonda, would henceforth be interlinked.

With these two in his portfolio, Brown had to redefine their respective aims while at the same time creating a synergy between them: sport in the case of Aston Martin, luxury in the case of Lagonda. At the London Motor Show in October 1948, there was a single stand under the Aston Martin & Lagonda insignia.

# LAGONDA

Wilbur Gunn was born in Springfield, Ohio in 1859. A stream runs through the town which the Shawnee Indians called Lagonda. Wilbur was the son of a Methodist pastor, and he inherited his father's strict attitude. Bored of choir and of chapel, he dreamed of new horizons. In his thirties, he gave up everything to move to Great Britain—everything except opera. He joined Carl Rosa's company and pursued a career as a tenor. He married Constance Grey, a woman of great subtlety, who bore him a daughter. He devoted himself more and more to his other passion, mechanics. He built a boat and tinkered with his first motorbikes. He moved to Staines, to the west of London, and founded the Lagonda Motor Cycle Co. Ltd on 18 May 1904. He progressed from two to three wheels with the Tricar and in 1907 built his first motor car.

Wilbur Gunn died in 1920, but the brand survived him. As economic conditions worsened, Lagonda was taken over by a consortium led by Alan Good. The new company, LG Motors (Staines) Ltd, was registered in August 1935. Alan Good immediately offered the technical directorship to Walter Owen Bentley, who had been unhappy about the takeover of his brand by Rolls-Royce Motors.

Alan Good decided to reposition the Lagonda image as top-of-the-range, but everything would be up for grabs again after the Second World War.

A Lagonda V12 Rapide designed by Frank Feeley, the designer of the first Aston Martins.

**Top:** The Atom prototype built in 1940 was not retained by David Brown. **Above:** The 2-litre Sports, victorious in the Spa 24 Hours in July 1948.

## The Atom Inherited (1940)

When David Brown bought Aston Martin, what were the assets he acquired? A brand that lived off the success of its sporting triumphs, modest premises on the outskirts of London and a prototype with an unprepossessing physique, the Atom saloon, completed in July 1940 and designed by the engineer Claude Hill, who had started his career in 1924 working alongside Bertelli.

Small and light, the Atom rested on a tubular chassis, to which an aluminium body was soldered. Two types of engines of similar capacity and power (2 litres, 90 hp), with or without overhead camshaft, were tested and connected to a Cotal pre-selective gearbox. This model didn't match David Brown's vision for Aston Martin; he wanted to revive its sporty image.

# The 2-Litre Sports Spa Model (1948)

David Brown asked his troops to produce a sportier prototype using the chassis and engine from the Atom. The bodywork took the form of a fuselage with the wheels anchored to the outside. The front was occupied by a vertical grille flanked by two small air intakes.

The 2-litre Sports (AMC/48/1 chassis, which would be numbered LMA/48/1 and then SPA/48/8) was completed in May 1948. It underwent tests in the hands of the engineer Claude Hill and the test driver John Horsfall. Then more seasoned drivers, like Freddie Dixon and Tony Rolt, took the wheel and were so impressed that they suggested to Claude Hill that he should enter the Spa 24 Hours race on 10 and 11 July 1948. Driven by Claude Hill and John Horsfall, the Aston Martin won the event, albeit against fairly mediocre opposition.

The 2-litre Sports was primed for the London Motor Show in October 1948, as racing cars were not admitted. It was put on sale under the name Spa Model or Spa Replica, but there were no takers.

The 2-litre Sports was offered for sale at Bonhams in 2015 in Carmel.

# The 2-Litre Sports Drophead Coupé (1948–1950)

At the same Motor Show in 1948, Aston Martin exhibited a second, and much more civilised, model. It was a convertible with a very sumptuous form created by Frank Feeley, who reprised certain stylistic tics of the Lagondas that he had designed before the war. This 2-litre Sports used the same mechanical base as the Spa car, this time connected to a David Brown gearbox. In less than two years, thirteen of these 2-litre Sports were built, and a fourteenth was delivered as a bare chassis.

The entire Aston Martin staff attend the birth of the 2-litre Sports DHC.

The DB Mark II no. LML/49/4 specially built for David Brown.

# THE METAMORPHOSES OF THE DB2

## The DB Mark II (1949)

The two versions of the 2-litre Sports got David Brown's adventure underway, but the entrepreneur had other ambitions. He planned a more finished model with a closed, comfortable and modern bodywork that would have its baptism of fire on the track. In early 1949, he launched the manufacture of three DB Mark II prototypes for the Le Mans 24 Hours. Frank Feeley had imagined a new style with flat sides and rectilinear belt line. Two of the cars used the four cylinders of the 2-litre Sports while the third (LML/48/3) introduced the new 2.6-litre six-cylinder dual overhead camshaft designed by William Watson under the supervision of W. O. Bentley:

- No. 19: chassis LML/49/3 (registration UMC66) for Charles Brackenbury and Leslie Johnson;

- No. 27: chassis LML/49/2 (UMC65) for Nick Haines and Arthur Jones;

- No. 28: chassis LML/49/1 (UMC64), Pierre Maréchal / T. A. S. O. Mathieson.

Only car no. 27 finished the race, in seventh place. No. 19 dropped out after just an hour, while no. 28 came off the track in the twenty-third hour, costing the life of Pierre Maréchal.

The two surviving DB Mark IIs were entered for the Spa 24 Hours and finished in third and fifth place.

David Brown had a fourth car (LML/49/4) prepared for his personal use. It had a distinctive red livery (not the almond green of the other three cars). Sold to the driver Lance Macklin in 1950, it raced in the Coppa Inter-Europa, the Targa Florio and the Mille Miglia. It survives to this day and last changed hands in 2017 at the Gooding auction house in Amelia Island for more than $1.5 million.

**Top:** The DB Mark II (no. LML/49/2), which took part in the Spa 24 Hours in July 1948. **Upper middle:** The physiognomy of the DB2 'washboard' at the start of its career on the LML/50/5 chassis. **Lower middle:** The first convertible using the DB2 (LML/50/10) chassis. **Above:** The DB2 in its final form, stripped of its side grilles and sporting a new radiator grille.

A DB2 Drophead Coupé (no. LML/50/237) in its second version, without the grills on its wings.

## The DB2 in Production (1950–1954)

There was never any DB1, though this apocryphal label was often wrongly attached to the 2-litre Sports. The DB2 label was attributed to the production version that first made an appearance at the New York Auto Show in April 1950. The front is fuller than on the racing cars, and the ground clearance is lower.

After the fiftieth unit (out of 309 coupés), the DB2 underwent various retouches: it lost the grilles along its sides that had earned it the nickname 'washboard'. The three-part radiator grille was replaced by one in a single piece, less angular and with horizontal bars.

The tenth unit of the DB2s (LML/50/10) was a convertible specially fitted for David Brown, the first in a series of 200. After January 1951, the Vantage option became available, with increased power of 125 hp.

In the transition from the DB2 to the DB2-4, the coupé here (no. LML/539 sold by Bonhams to Goodwood for nearly $300,00 in 2020) lost none of its elegance, especially in its wonderful almond-green livery.

## The DB2-4 Becomes Respectable (1953–1955)

The DB2 was superseded by the DB2-4 in October 1953. Its seating capacity was increased from two to four seats thanks to a modification of the design of the passenger compartment, which now had a hunchback profile. A tailgate incorporating the rear window allowed easier access to the luggage compartment.

The bodywork was produced by Mulliners, a Birmingham firm not to be confused with the similar-sounding Arthur Mulliner and H. J. Mulliner. A long-established company, it began as a harness maker in the nineteenth century. The final assembly took place in the Farsley factory near Leeds in Yorkshire, where David Brown's tractors were produced.

At first, the DB2-4 was driven by a VB6E engine (2.6 litres, 125 hp), which was comparable to the Vantage used in the DB2. From April 1954, it used the VB6J (2.9 litres, 140 hp).

The DB2-4 was available as a coupé (Saloon, 451 units) and as a convertible (Drophead Coupé, 102 units).

# THE DB2-4 IN *THE BIRDS*

It was an Aston Martin DB2-4 that Tippi Hedren was driving when she arrived at the Potter School in Bodega Bay in Alfred Hitchcock's *The Birds*. A long panning shot followed the convertible as it drove along the Pacific Highway and through the village. The car had the LML/944 chassis and was rented by Universal Studios to use in the 1963 film.

The arrival of the DB2-4 DHC at the Potter School in Hitchcock's *The Birds*.

Aston Martins always came in subtle colours, like this DB2-4 convertible no. LML/829.

# THE ITALIAN LOOK

Several cars in the DB2 family have served as the basis for artisanal work elsewhere. In the early 1950s, Italian coachbuilders sought to establish agreements with manufacturers to produce their marginal series, while at the same time continuing to produce one-off items and custom-made bodyworks. Here is a selection.

**Top:** The voluptuous contours designed by Franco Scaglione for the DB2-4 no. LML/505. **Middle:** DB2-4 no. LML/504 convertible designed by Michelotti and executed by Bertone in 1953. **Above:** A DB2-4 'Indiana' convertible which was styled by Scaglione and built in 1954 by Bertone.

### DB2-4 LML/502, 505 and 507
### Racing Spider by Bertone, 1953

Stanley Harold 'Wacky' Arnolt was a Chicago-based millionaire who wanted to distribute customised British cars in the United States. He purchased a job lot of bare chassis from Aston Martin which he handed over to Bertone. Three cars were given bodyworks in the expressive style of Franco Scaglione. An engineer and aeronaut and later fashion stylist, Scaglione was one of the most innovative figures in Italian bodywork design.

### DB2-4 no. LML/504 and 506
### Convertible by Bertoni, 1953

Wacky Arnolt again made two other convertibles, this time in a more classical, somewhat staid style by Giovanni Michelotti. The first convertible was paid for by the employees of the Brown & Birgelow company as a gift to their boss, benefactor and former convict!

### DB2-4 LML/761
### Coupé by Carrozzeria Allemano, 1953

A one-off car produced by J. O'Hara, a friend of David Brown living in Casablanca. As well as its special bodywork designed by Giovanni Savonuzzi, this DB2-4 was equipped with an engine with features similar to those used in the DB3.

### DB2-4 no. LML/762
### 'Indiana' convertible by Bertone, 1954

Another car financed by Wacky Arnolt, this time for his personal use. Designed by Scaglione, it is distinguished by its panoramic windscreen.

### DB2-4 no. LML/765
### Coupé by Bertone, 1957

Another commission by Stanley Arnolt. Designed once more by Franco Scaglione, this car was exhibited by Bertone at the Turin Car Show in October 1957 and November 1958.

### DB2-4 no. LML/802
### Coupé by Vignale, 1955

Delivered to King Badouin of Belgium in March 1955, this coupé echoes the style of the Ferrari 250 Europa GT no. 0359/GT made for Liliale de Réthy, his mother-in-law. The two cars were designed by Giovanni Michelotti and executed by Vignale.

### DB2-4 Mark II no. AM300/1132
### 'Supersonic' coupé by Ghia, 1956

The 'Supersonic' bodywork, inspired by aviation, is the work of Giovanni Savonuzzi, who was an aircraft engineer before becoming technical director at Cisitalia and later Ghia. This style was reproduced on thirteen Fiat 8Vs, three Jaguar XK 120s, one Alfa Romeo 1900 Sprint and one Aston Martin. It was exhibited at the Turin Car Show in April 1956 before being delivered to the race driver Harry Schell.

### DB2-4 Mark II no. AM300/1161, 1162 and 1163
### Spider by Touring Superleggera, 1956

The simple and balanced lines of these spiders reveal the mastery of Federico Formenti of Touring. The chassis no. 1162 was displayed at the Paris Car Show in 1956.

**Top:** The Supersonic contour applied to the DB2-4 by Ghia. **Upper middle:** The DB2-4 coupé made by Vignale for the King of Belgium. **Lower middle:** The DB2-4 coupé displayed by Bertone at the 1957 Turin Car Show. **Above:** The DB2-4 chassis by Touring on the Aston Martin stand at the Paris Car Show in 1956.

The chrome strips help to identify the DB2-4 Mark II.

# The DB2-4 Mark II (1955–1957)

The launch of the DB2-4 Mark II at the London Motor Show in 1955 came at a time when the company was making changes to their mode of production. In 1953, David Brown bought the coachmaker Tickford Ltd, who were based in Newport Pagnell, in workshops occupied by Salmons & Sons since 1820! The DB2-4 Mark II would therefore be manufactured by Tickford and no longer by Mulliners. The mechanics were little changed— the 3-litre 140 hp engine was as before, though a special series delivering 165 hp was also available. On the outside, the Mark II was identifiable by its raised passenger compartment, the more prominent fins and the chrome strips attached to the wings and under the framework.

Alongside the coupé (Saloon) and the convertible (Drophead Coupé), a third type of bodywork was introduced: a hard-top coupé with a projecting boot (Fixed Head Coupé) which created a 'notchback' profile.

The prototype (LML/515) was made by Mulliners from a convertible, but the series models were manufactured by Tickford.

The output of the DB2-4 Mark II consisted of 135 coupés (Saloon), thirty-four hard-top coupés (FHC), twenty-four convertibles (DHC) and four bare chassis. The novelist Françoise Sagan was one of the few people to own a convertible, but unfortunately, speeding too fast, she had a terrible accident on 13 April 1957 near Milly-la-Forêt while driving this car.

The DB Mark III exhibited at the London Motor Show in 1957.

## The DB Mark III (1957–1958)

The third phase of the evolution of the DB2-4, which began in March 1957, was known commercially simply as the DB Mark III. It was substantially modified, more reliable, safer and faster, with a top speed of more than 190 km/h. The most visible change was the adoption of an improved radiator grille, inspired by the one on the DB3 S. The dashboard was streamlined, with all the dials facing the driver.

The engine was modified by the engineer Tadek Marek, who had joined Aston Martin in 1954 from Austin. The power was increased from 162 hp with a single (DBA type) exhaust to 180 hp with a double (DBD) exhaust and to 195 hp with three carburettors. The clutch and gearbox were revised to support a higher torque and a Laycock overdrive was available as an option. On the first 100 cars, front disc brakes were still an option, but with chassis no. 1401 they were installed as standard.

The price list included the coupé (Saloon), 462 units, and the convertible (DHC), still a collector's item at only eighty-four units, while the hard-top coupé (FHC) was made on demand with a DBD engine for five privileged customers.

The DB Mark III would be produced at Newport Pagnell until July 1959, nine months after the launch of the DB4, which would remain sought after for a very long time.

**Above:** The DB Mark III Drophead Coupé no. AMR300/3/1700 sold by RM Sotheby's in Monterey in 2011. **Opposite:** A DB Mark III Drophead Coupé in a subtle shade of green, Aston Martin's fetish colour.

# DAVID BROWN ON THE RACETRACK

David Brown wanted to reinvigorate the sporting fibre that was in the DNA of Aston Martin. Participating in the Le Mans 24 Hours between 1949 and 1951 with the DB Mark II and the DB2 was just a rehearsal. Brown soon set to work on a truly competitive machine to fulfil his ambitions.

The DB3-1 transformed into a coupé for the 1952 Le Mans 24 Hours.

**Above left:** The DB3 driven by Reg Parnell in July 1953 at Silverstone. **Above right:** This strange coupé on a DB3-7 chassis was bought by Angela Brown, David's daughter, in 1954.

# The DB3 (1951–1952)

In 1950, John Wyer was appointed as team manager of David Brown Racing. A distinguished man of forty-one, he had served his apprenticeship at Sunbeam, and then had worked at Solex and Monaco Motors for his friend Dudley Folland. In November 1950, Brown appointed the German engineer Robert Eberan von Eberhorst as technical director; he had previously collaborated with Ferdinand Porsche on his single-seater Auto-Union Type D and Cisitalia 360.

The engineer wanted to keep it simple: so the chassis was a conventional one, consisting of a ladder frame with large-diameter tubes. The de Dion rear axle was suspended by torsion bars.

David Brown wanted the DB3's debut to be at the Le Mans 24 Hours in 1951, but they weren't ready in time and he had to resort to the DB2. One of them finished third overall, with a victory in its class.

It wasn't until September 1951 that the DB3 got its first run-out at the Tourist Trophy in Dundrod. Three new cars were built during that winter and competed at Silverstone in 1952. The DB3's weaknesses were revealed: it was too heavy and, at 133 hp, not powerful enough. Three of them started the Le Mans 24 Hours in 1952, but none of them stayed the course: no. 25 (DB3-5) for Peter Collins and Lance Macklin, no. 26 (DB3-3) for Pat Griffith and Dennis Poore and no. 28 (DB3-1) for Reg Parnell and Eric Thomson, the latter choosing a hard-top to achieve higher speeds. For the rest of the season, the DB3 used a more powerful (163 hp) 3-litre engine, and it chalked up its first win that August at Goodwood.

Despite the lack of results, Aston Martin managed to sell five DB3s to its customers, two of which were special coupés, which supplemented the four factory cars and a road model built for David Brown's personal use.

A rare pearl: one of the three DB3 S coupés prepared for the road.

# The DB3 S (1953–1955)

David Brown drew some conclusions from this mixed season for the DB3: he had to come up with a lighter, more powerful car. The incumbent German engineer was not of the same mind, and he was replaced by William Watson. At the start of the 1953 season, Aston Martin was still racing with the DB3 and attained a creditable second place at the Sebring 12 Hours.

Finally ready in May 1953, the new DB3 S possessed a six-cylinder 2.9-litre engine which had been reworked to deliver 182 hp of power, subsequently 225 hp with double ignition. Made of aluminium, the DB3 S was 75 kg lighter than the DB3, and the geometry of its rear suspension had been revised. The tubular chassis was more compact, and the design of the bodywork, still Frank Feeley's department, had been refined. The voluptuous profile was marked by the wheel arch, which formed a deeply indented scoop.

The DB3 S evolved over the course of its sporting career. The front braking system would be supplied with discs. The grille would be refined, then become larger between two profiled headlights. For the 1954 season, two magnificent coupés were constructed (DB3 S-6 and 7) and entered in the Le Mans 24 Hours (one of them was fitted with a compressor, which raised the power to 240 hp). They came off the road and would end up rebuilt as open-top sports prototypes. Three similar coupés (nos. 113, 119 and 120) were constructed for more gentle pursuits.

Top left: The sales catalogue for the original DB3 S. Top right: Stirling Moss in the DB3 S-5 at Goodwood in 1956.
Above: The DB3 S-9 in its last incarnation, entered for the Le Mans 24 Hours in 1956.

Aston Martin manufactured around thirty DB3 Ss, of which about ten were reserved for the factory while the other twenty were taken on by private ecuries. Commercialised at the London Motor Show of 1954, the DB3 S had a price tag of £3,684 (or £4,800 for the coupé).

The DB3 S distinguished itself in the national trials but not in the rounds that counted towards the World Championship. At the Le Mans 24 Hours it finished second on three separate occasions: in 1955 (with Peter Collins and Paul Frère), 1956 (with Peter Collins and Stirling Moss) and 1958 (with Graham and Peter Whitehead).

# TED CUTTING, ENGINEER

The engineer responsible for the DBR1, Edward John Cutting (1926–2012), is not well known among the general public. Immersed in the motor world from a very early age—his father was a salesman and his uncle a racing mechanic at Napier—he worked for KLG Spark Plugs and Allard before blossoming at Aston Martin.

First outing of the DBR1 at the Le Mans 24 Hours in March 1956.

## The DBR1 (1956–1960)

In 1956, David Brown set to work on a new car to replace the DB3 S. For this DBR1, the engineer Ted Cutting designed a whole new chassis, made up of a trellis of fine tubes. Made rigid, it weighed in at 23 kg lighter than that of the DB3 S. The DBR1 benefitted from a de Dion rear-wheel axle unit, but at the front it kept the suspension of the DB3 S with its transversal torsion bars.

The bodywork too was a refinement of that of the DB3 S. The six-cylinder 2.5-litre engine (DBR1-250) with double ignition now had a light alloy block and produced 240 hp. Things changed in 1957, when the DBR1 moved up to 3 litres (DBR1-300). Initially, the valves were arranged at an angle of 60° and from August the opening of the V changed to 95°, which resulted in a significant improvement in performance. In 1957, the DBR1 driven by Noel Cunningham-Reid outpaced the DBR1-2 at the Nürburgring.

**Above left:** The DBR2-1 made for the Le Mans 24 Hours in 1957. **Above right:** The Aston Martin team before the start of the Le Mans 24 Hours in 1958.

The regulations for sports prototypes were changed for the 1958 season, and their capacity was limited to 3 litres. This was to Aston Martin's advantage, as it put a number of their competitors out of the picture, notably the Jaguar D-Type and the Maserati 450 S. The DBR1 won the German round again, this time with Jack Brabham and Stirling Moss in the DBR1-3. On the other hand, they had a nightmare at Le Mans, when not a single DBR1 finished the race! Nevertheless, Aston Martin finished runner-up to Ferrari in the sports car class of the World Championship.

The year of 1959 was one of consecration, with Aston Martin claiming three victories in the last three rounds of the season: Jack Fairman / Stirling Moss at the Nürburgring (DBR1-1), Carroll Shelby / Roy Salvadori at the Le Mans 24 Hours (DBR1-2), and Jack Fairman / Stirling Moss / Carroll Shelby at the Tourist Trophy (DBR1-2).

The four factory cars and the private DBR1 of Whitehead all raced at Le Mans. Faster (thanks to a higher compression ratio), Moss's DBR1-3 played the role of the hare in the first hours of the race.

Aston Martin constructed only five cars of the DBR1 type for three seasons of racing. Only one was ever sold, the DBR1-5 entrusted to Graham Whitehead.

# The DBR2 (1957)

For the Le Mans 24 Hours of 1957 Aston Martin produced a DBR2, which differed from the DBR1 by being fitted with a 3.7-litre engine, which prefigured that of the DB4, and by its beam frame derived from the Lagonda V12 of 1955. Stirling Moss drove a DBR2 in the Nassau Tourist Trophy and the Governor's Trophy, then it was fitted with a 3.9-litre engine which helped Tony Brooks to net second place in the British Empire Trophy, but a new limitation of 3 litres in 1958 disqualified the DBR2, which was confined to competing in non-championship races in Britain or America. The two existing DBR2s emigrated to the United States, where their capacity was increased even further to 4.2 litres.

# A Brief Flirtation with Formula 1 (1959)

Aston Martin has always been somewhat circumspect when it comes to Formula 1, with the exception of one appearance in 1959. Aston Martin entered the ring with the DBR4, which seemed to be outmoded from the start. While it was known that the regulations would change in 1961, with the reduction in capacity from 2.5 litres to 1.5 litres, and there was pressure to establish the central engine more widely, Aston Martin came up with a magnificent single-seater, but one which seemed like a dinosaur with its front engine, a six-cylinder extrapolated from the block of the DBR1. The best results were obtained by Roy Salvadori in 1959: sixth in Britain and Portugal; Carroll Shelby was eighth in Portugal.

# CARROLL SHELBY

One of the drivers who achieved victory for Aston Martin in the Le Mans 24 Hours was an all-American boy. Born 11 January 1923 in Leesburg, Texas, Carroll Shelby was the archetypical cowboy: strong, happy-go-lucky and a bit rough around the edges. Europe was first introduced to his greying shock of hair and craggy features in June 1959 at Le Mans. He was a dilettante as a driver, but brilliant, and he won the 24 Hours alongside Roy Salvadori at the wheel of an Aston Martin DBR1.

Previously, Carroll Shelby had stood out particularly at Sebring 12 Hours in 1955, where he finished as runner-up with Phil Hill in a Ferrari 750 Monza. He also made a few appearances in the Formula 1 World Championship at the wheel of a Maserati 250 F of the Scuderia Centro Sud in 1958 and of an Aston Martin DBR4 in 1959. After this, Shelby hung up his crash helmet and began a career as a constructor with an ingenious idea: to turn a modest British roadster into a little monster, in other words, transform the AC Ace into a furious Cobra. On 10 May 2012, Carroll Shelby had his final pit stop, at the age of eighty-nine.

Victory at Le Mans in 1959 was one of Carroll Shelby's greatest successes as a driver.

# STIRLING MOSS, CHAMPION WITHOUT A CROWN

The reputation stuck to him throughout his life: Stirling Moss was one of the greatest drivers of his era but never achieved the title of world champion. He passed away on 12 April 2020.

Moss made his debut at the age of nineteen in the seat of a Cooper-JAP, after which driving became his principal activity. As a young man, he showed admirable patriotism by driving single-seaters produced by smaller British workshops: Connaught, HWM or ERA. He had no reward for this sacrifice, but at least got himself noticed by Lofty England, the sporting director of Jaguar, who engaged him for the Le Mans 24 Hours. His career took off in 1954, and in the following year he joined the Mercedes-Benz team alongside Juan Manuel Fangio. By chance, Moss's sole victory came at Aintree, in front of the British public, but that did nothing to take away his reputation as the eternal runner-up. For four years in a row, 1955 to 1958, he would be vice-champion of the world, and between 1959 and 1961 he would be in third place! In 1957, the Union Jack reminded Moss of his patriotic duty, and he was recruited by the British ecurie Vanwall. In 1958 and 1959 he was part of David Brown's official team. On 15 April 1962, the insatiable Moss raced in the Glover Trophy at Goodwood. The UDT-Laystall Racing team gave him a Lotus 18, in which he clocked up the fastest time in qualifying. During the race, having been delayed by a gearbox problem, he fought his way aggressively back into contention. On the thirty-fifth lap he came off the track at the St Mary corner and crashed into the embankment. One year later, after months in a coma and a painful convalescence, Stirling Moss was back at the wheel. But his heart was no longer in it, and his passion and talent had waned too.

**Top:** Stirling Moss, Formula 1 vice-champion of the world from 1955 to 1958. **Above:** The DBR4 had a superb lineage, but was technologically outmoded.

The DB4 Series V in the Vantage version with its profiled headlights similar to those on the DB4 GT.

# DB4, 5, 6:
# THE ITALIAN FIRM

There was a change of tone after the DB2 and the DB2-4: this time Aston Martin turned to an Italian bodywork manufacturer to design its next generation.

Italian bodywork really took off after the Second World War. It imposed its style on the whole world. In a few dazzling lines it swept away the now old-fashioned, mannered look of the French, which had dominated in the 1930s. This blossoming of the Latin look came to rival the exuberant styling of Americans that had so fascinated consumers at the cusp of the 1930s. The world of Italian bodywork was dominated by two leading figures who expressed their personalities and cultivated their differences throughout the 1950s: Pinin Farina, the defender of the classical approach, and Bertone, who favoured a more avant-garde attitude. On the fringes of this great rivalry, a number of other businesses ploughed their own furrow. Notable among them was Carrozzeria Touring Superleggera, which managed to impose its very refined style on both these rivals.

The DP114 project developed in-house was fortunately abandoned.

# THE DB4: AN ICON
# IN FIVE ACTS (1958–1963)

After a sequence of respectable, elegant, quintessentially British sports cars—the DB2, the DB2-4 and the DB Mark III—Aston Martin decided to move away from its home-grown style and employ the services of a quality Italian maker.

The launch of the DB4 in October 1958 marked a big departure. For the first time in the history of the brand a model officially listed in the catalogue could no longer claim to belong fully to British culture. In an act of lèse-majesté, Aston Martin had the audacity to turn to Carrozzeria Touring to tailor the finishing touches to the new DB4. And this, after having developed its own proposal, under the reference DP114, and after having, fortunately, rejected it.

# FEDERICO FORMENTI:
# THE UNSUNG HERO OF TOURING

The stylist Federico Formenti remained in the shadows; he is pictured here behind this Pagaso Thrill in the centre of this team grouping.

At Carrozzeria Touring it was Federico Formenti, working behind the scenes, who set the tone. Italian bodywork companies have always had the annoying habit of disguising the identity of the stylists to whom they owe their fame. In all their offices, the names of their creative talents are hidden. Even if the creator's signatures sometimes appear at the base of the designs, the companies rarely publicise them. The tradition was that the name of the enterprise should be highlighted—often the surname of the owner. This was the case with Zagato, Bertone and Pinin Farina. The same attitude persisted at Touring, where Carlo Bianchi Anderloni had no compunction in co-signing the sketches made by Federico Formenti. However, most of the directors of the large firms did not themselves design. Their artistic skill consisted in picking out the talented stylists who would be able to interpret their will. This was the case with Felice Bianchi Anderloni, who engaged Federico Formenti a short time after he took up the reins at Touring.

Federico Formenti (1925–1995) was always overshadowed by the personality of his boss. Stylist, draftsman-designer and talented illustrator, he carried the flame of the two artists who occupied the drawing board one after the other before the war: G. Seregni and G. Belli. Formenti gave form to such monuments as the Ferrari 166 Mille Miglia, the Lancia Flaminia GT and the Pegaso Z-102. He consistently breathed elegance and purity into his creations by means of pared-back lines and simple forms. When Touring shut up shop in January 1967, Formenti would work for the bodymaker Marazzi and would design the Islero for Lamborghini.

The Alfa Romeo 2000 Spider developed by Touring at the same time as the Aston Martin DB4.

**Top:** Standard attached the name of Vignale to this Vanguard model. **Above:** The highly innovative Austin A 40 was conceived in close collaboration with Pinin Farina.

# TOURING: A MAJOR NAME IN ITALIAN BODYWORK

Carrozzeria Touring was founded in 1926 by Felice Bianchi Anderloni, who was born in Rome in 1883. Throughout the 1930s, the firm established its reputation by creating elegant bodyworks, notably on the magnificent theme of the 'Flying Star'. On the eve of the Second World War, Touring distinguished itself from its contemporaries by the modernity of its construction, its sports cars being manufactured using the Superleggera method, which was based on a trellis of thin tubes to which aluminium plates were attached.

When Anderloni died in 1948, he was succeeded as head of the enterprise by his son Carlo Felice, who had been working for the company for three years. (An engineer by training, he was born in Milan on 7 April 1916.) At this time, Touring faced the same problem as all the other firms: how to survive the standardisation of production. They decided to offer a design service as well as production.

In the 1950s, the Latin wind would reach as far as the UK. The British constructors turned more and more to the Italians as they sought to modernise their image. To create the ingenious Austin A 40, a cross between an estate car and a saloon, and the more conventional Austin Cambridge, the British Motor Corporation solicited the aid of Pinin Farina (spelt as two words until 1961). The management at Standard Triumph, to get away from their somewhat staid style, turned to Giovanni Michelotti and his partner Vignale to create the Standard Vanguard saloon in 1956 and subsequently to design numerous Triumphs between 1950 and 1970, from the Herald to the Stag via the Spitfire and the TR 4. It was in this same spirit that Aston Martin Lagonda consulted Touring to make a break with the past and imagine its new generation of DB4 coupés and its Rapide saloon. After this, Touring manufactured small series of 145 units of the Sunbeam Venezia for the Rootes group.

Presented at the Turin Car Show in 1963, the Sunbeam Venezia was produced in a limited series by Carrozzeria Touring.

# TADEK MAREK

At Newport Pagnell in 1958, the workshop dedicated to the manufacture of the new six-cylinder engine designed by Tadek Marek.

Tadeusz (Tadek) Marek (1908–1982) is famous for having created two engines that were quintessential in the evolution of Aston Martin: the six-cylinder engine of the DB4, previously pencilled in for the DBR2, and the V8 of the DBS. Of Polish origin (he was born in Cracow), he studied in Berlin before being taken on first by Fiat and then by General Motors. He fled to Britain during the war, and after the Liberation spent a few years in Germany in the service of the United Nations. Marek worked for Austin between 1949 and 1954 before being hired by Aston Martin.

In Touring's more purified style, the DB4 was characterised by its rectilinear profile and its smooth surfaces. The mechanics also harboured some interesting surprises. A new in-line six-cylinder engine with double overhead camshaft was created by the engineer Tadek Marek.

The DB4 would undergo five phases of evolution. The second series of the DB4 appeared from February 1960. This Series II was not much different apart from some adjustments to the braking system (adoption of larger-diameter discs than previously) and to the lubrification (installing a larger-capacity oil sump). The list of options grew larger with electric window lifts and an overdrive made available. On the outside, the Series II was distinguishable only in a few details: the slightly thicker bumpers and the chrome surrounds on the windows.

Aston Martin introduced a third series of the DB4 in April 1961. Once again, the modifications really only touched on points of details on the inside: an electric tachometer on the dashboard and a more efficient demisting system. On the outside, the only distinctive sign was the round tail-lights embedded in a chrome casing.

The fourth instalment in the DB4 series arrived in September 1961. There were only fairly timid modifications to the bodywork. Why would you want to change the superb contours of the Touring design? Nevertheless the radiator grille was made heavier with the addition of vertical bars, the rear lights were replaced by vertical elements, and the air intake on the engine was flattened. Inside the passenger compartment, smokers will have noticed that the ashtray had changed place. It is with this fourth series that a useful Vantage option first appeared on the price list.

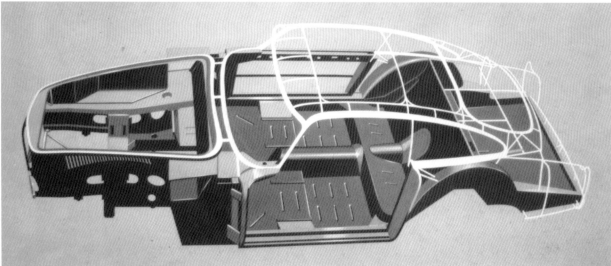

**Top:** The DB4 in its very first configuration. **Above:** Touring's Superleggera structure designed for the DB4.

Thanks to three SU HD8 carburettors in place of the normal two, the power increased effortlessly from 240 to 260 hp at 5,570 rpm. Most of the Vantage DB4s were given profiled headlights, in the image of the DB4 GT, but their wheelbase remained the same as that of the regular DB4s.

**Top left:** A new radiator grille, vertical rear lights and a flat air intake were the distinguishing features of the DB4 Series IV.
**Top right:** The DB4 Series V in its Vantage version, with its profiled headlights similar to those on the DB4 GT.
**Above:** Series II of the DB4 (no. 463/R) with its distinctive chrome trim around the windows.

The fifth and last instalment of the DB4 series went on sale in September 1962. The bodywork was extended by 9 cm to improve the boot capacity and the roof was slightly raised, prefiguring an evolution towards a more comfortable style of coupé. But the retouches were done discreetly and did not distract from the overall aesthetics of the car. The DB4 adopted the dashboard that was previously reserved for the DB4 GT, with separate dials for oil pressure, water temperature, fuel gauge and battery charge.

Most of the Series V DB4s were commissioned with the Vantage option, which could draw upon 266 hp. For more sporty types, it was possible to substitute the DB GT engine, which provided 302 hp. Such shock treatment was applied to only six cars. And thus came to an end the story of the DB4, the epitome of the Aston Martin spirit.

The choice of the DB4 for Jules Dassin's 1962 film *Phaedra* was not merely random. In this parable of desire, it is the car that Phaedra (Melina Mercouri) offers to her son-in-law Alexis (Anthony Perkins), with whom she is madly in love. It is also at the wheel of the magnificent silver-grey coupé that the young man throws himself from the top of a cliff to bring this tragedy to a brutal conclusion. Rest assured, the car used for the scene was a simple Sunbeam in disguise!

# LA BERLINE DB4,
# ALIAS LAGONDA RAPIDE

First shown at the London Motor Show in 1961, the Lagonda Rapide was a thoroughbred among saloons which had the same basic mechanics as the DB4, notably its engine (inline six-cylinders, 3,995 cc, 236 hp at 5,000 rpm). Its structure rested on a steel platform derived from that of the DB4 but with the wheelbase extended to 289 cm. The running gear consisted of a de Dion rear axle, coil springs at the front and torsion bars at the rear. The style is pure Touring, marrying the classic elegance of a smart saloon with the sporting character that was intrinsic to their roots. Despite its pedigree and its qualities on the road, the Lagonda Rapide remained a private affair. Only fifty-five were produced, and production ended in 1964.

**Above:** The Lagonda Rapide could have become the archetype of the ideal roadster. **Following pages:** The profile of the DB4 series in all its purity.

The second series of the DB4 Convertible (1962, like the 1099/L) was equipped with deflectors.

## The DB4 Convertible (1961–1963)

A superb new convertible built on the base of the DB4 was unveiled at the Paris Car Show of 1961. The coupé was even more pure of line than the drop-top version. The DB4 Convertible followed on the evolution of the DB4 Saloon, the first series of the Convertible corresponding to the fourth series of the now-terminated version.

When the DB4 Saloon Series V appeared in September 1962, the Convertible was only in its second manifestation: it was made slightly longer, and its dashboard was revamped. Unlike the coupé, the Convertible was fitted with deflectors.

In total, seventy-nine DB4 Convertibles were distributed, of which forty-five belonged to the second series. Thirty-two cars had the Vantage engine, which provided 266 hp as opposed to the 240 hp of the standard model.

## THE DB4 GT JET

Nineteen DB4 GT chassis were sent to Zagato, and a twentieth to Bertone. Built on chassis no. 0201, this coupé, baptised 'Jet', was designed by Giorgetto Giugiaro in a style that is at once gracious and muscular, with all reference to Aston Martin erased.

The DB4 GT Jet designed by Giorgetto Giugiaro for Bertone.

# The Very Rare DB4 GT (1959–1961)

The Aston Martin DB4 provided the platform for a new sporting policy. After the 1959 season, Aston Martin quit the World Endurance Championship at the top and refocused on the Grand Touring category with the DB4 GT and its derivatives. The first prototype of the DB4 GT (DP199 type) made a discreet appearance at the Le Mans 24 Hours in June 1959, but its debut passed largely unnoticed alongside the five DBR1s which were racing for victory. Moreover, the DB4 GT, driven by Jacques Calderari and Hubert Patthey, would be forced to retire to general indifference after twenty-one hours of racing.

The DB4 GT was officially added to the commercial range from October 1959. Compared to the DB4, it was shorter, lighter and better profiled. It was mounted on a chassis with a wheelbase reduced from 249 to 236 cm, which made its silhouette more compact while its general contours preserved the general style defined by Touring. The headlights were profiled as on the DB4 Vantage. The power of the six-cylinder engine had increased from 267 to 331 hp thanks to three Weber carburettors which replaced the two SUs of the regular version. Sharper brake performance was provided by the Girling discs, which replaced the Dunlops and didn't require assistance, as this was considered incompatible with properly sharp sports driving. A limited-slip differential was fitted as standard.

The DB4 GT would remain a limited edition of seventy-five cars, to which Zagato's fabulous version would be added.

Built on a shortened wheelbase, the DB4 GT (here 0104/L) looked more compact than the DB4.

The DB5 is instantly recognisable by its headlights encased inside profiled globes, as on the DB4 Vantages.

# THE DB5: JAMES BOND AND BEYOND (1963–1965)

The transition from the DB4 to the DB5 took place smoothly in July 1963. In terms of aesthetics, the bodywork of the DB5 merely applied the results of the experiments on the DB4 Vantage, in particular by adopting headlights placed under Plexiglas profiling. The only other visible difference was in the fuel filler, which had been doubled.

The engine, on the other hand had undergone major modifications. Capacity had increased from 3,670 to 3,995 cc by increasing the bore. The power made a leap from 240 to 282 hp. In view of this, the Vantage version would no longer be an option in the short term. The four-speed gearbox came as standard with overdrive, but it was already possible to get a five-speed ZF gearbox or a Borg Warner automatic transmission. Note the installation of an alternator instead of the dynamo.

In the autumn of 1964, the DB5 produced its second and final vintage. Now, the five-speed gearbox was fitted as standard. And the Vantage option reappeared in the catalogue: thanks to three Weber carburettors, the 4-litre engine now provided 314 hp at 5,750 rpm.

Despite its short lifespan, the DB5 was acquired by 1,023 buyers, of whom 200 chose the Vantage option.

# AN ICONOCLASTIC SHOOTING BRAKE

In the past, there was the Chevrolet Nomad, a concept car born in 1954 from the transformation of the Corvette roadster into an estate car. The idea was always in the air. The desire to transform the utilitarian image of the estate car is a recurrent one among designers, but not very many projects manage to turn the fantasy into reality.

However, at the Paris Car Show in October 1964, Aston Martin exhibited their DB5, which they had baptised the 'Shooting Brake'. The story was that it was David Brown himself who had the idea. Annoyed that he was unable to stash his polo gear and tired of his dog dirtying the leather seats of his coupé, he drew up some specifications to create a space where the dog could sit.

It is the convention to call this type of sporty estate car a 'shooting brake'. But the origin of the term is obscure. In the nineteenth century, it was a utilitarian horse-drawn carriage, uncovered, with the coachman installed at the front on a raised seat. The vehicle was probably intended to be used for hunting, as the name suggests. The origin of the word 'brake' is uncertain, but it was another word for 'bridle', the device used to slow a horse down, and so giving rise to the modern usage of the word 'brake'. But the similar word 'break' is also used to apply to the training of a horse.

Whatever the case, Aston Martin gave the name of 'Shooting Brake' to a special DB5 put together by the bodywork maker Harold Radford, who would make a total of twelve hunting estate cars based on the DB5, including four with left-hand drive.

The DB5 Shooting Brake exhibited at the Paris Car Show in 1964.

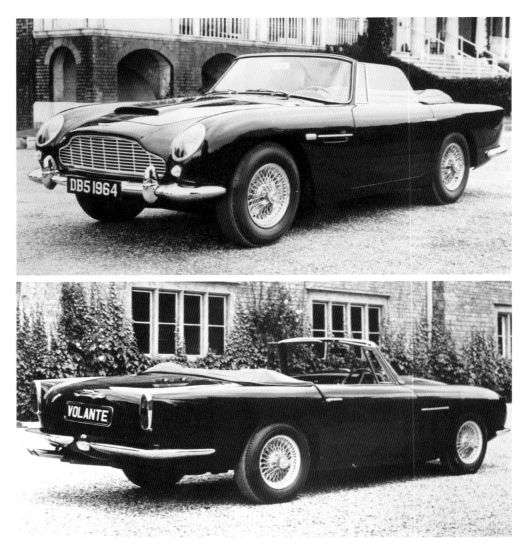

**Top:** The first version of the DB5 Convertible, 1964 vintage. **Above:** In October 1965, the Volante was no longer fully a DB5, nor was it a DB6.

## From the Convertible to the Volante (1963–1966)

When the DB5 started racing, in July 1963, its convertible version was down on the race list alongside the saloon. The two models would happily co-exist, but the convertible was much less sought after, despite its superb contours (123 cars produced between 1963 and 1965).

When the DB6 was brought in in October 1965, only a coupé (saloon) version was envisaged. The convertible didn't go down the DB6 route; it didn't adopt the longer chassis and continued to be based on the DB5 with its wheelbase of 2.49 m. However, so as not to appear a relic from the past, the convertible dropped any reference to the DB5 and called itself simply the 'Volante'. It adopted the same front face as the DB6 Saloon with the two-part bumper and the additional air intake, but not the truncated rear highlighted by a spoiler. This halfway house between the DB5 and the DB6 was little in demand (only thirty-seven were ever produced).

# DP212, 214 AND 215 (1962–1963)

In 1962, an Aston Martin lined up at the start of the Le Mans 24 Hours competing in the category labelled 'experimental'. Unlike the 'sport' category, which limited the capacity of the prototypes to 3 litres, this classification, specific to Le Mans, allowed engines up to 4 litres. The Aston Martin DP212 presented itself in the form of a coupé that could be commercialised … but wasn't. Hence its classification as experimental. Built on a DB4 GT base, the DP212 used a six-cylinder 4-litre engine. Driven by Graham Hill and Richie Ginther, this superb coupé proved to be very speedy, but had to drop out after six hours of racing.

This GT-like prototype demonstrated the confusion that the sport found itself in. In 1962, the Fédération Internationale de l'Automobile imposed new rules: the constructors' world championship was open to 'grand touring' cars and no longer 'sports' cars. To achieve ratification, at least a hundred units of a GT had to be produced in a given year. But one small paragraph in the rules sowed the seeds of trouble: a clause allowed a GT car to have a special bodywork, different from that of the officially approved car, provided that it was anchored to the chassis at the same points, wasn't any lighter than the approved model and maintained the same levels of comfort and habitability. This left the door wide open to multiple interpretations, excesses and dodgy tricks. Suddenly there was a plethora of GTs that had the appearance of prototypes: Cobra Daytona, Ferrari 250 GTO, Alfa Romeo TZ 2.

In 1963, at Le Mans, Aston Martin lined up with three cars that seemed identical: however, the DP215-1 no. 18 of Graham Hill and Lucien Bianchi was a prototype, whereas the two DP214s (no. 7 for William Kimberley and Joseph Schlesser and no. 8 for Innes Ireland and Bruce McLaren) were admitted as GTs. These two cars had the chassis number of the DB4 GT (0194/R and 0195/R respectively), while the DP215-1 was registered as a 'prototype'. The main difference between the two models concerned the engine: the one in the DP215 being a 4-litre dry sump developing 326 at 5,800 rpm. Moreover, the DP215 was slightly lighter.

The three Aston Martins dropped out of the race in 1963; the DP214 no. 0194/R raced again in 1964 (no. 18 Michael Salmon / Peter Sutcliffe), but was disqualified.

The magnificent DP215, sold for $21,450,000 by RM Sotheby's in Monterey in 2018.

# OF OTHER SHOOTING BRAKES

The small number of shooting brakes that were built on the base of the DB5 inspired a handful of original customers to order similar transformations to the DB6. The bodywork maker Harold Radford, the author of the DB5, was called upon again. He had been set up in South Kensington since the 1940s, and he had always specialised in converting saloons into shooting brakes. He was therefore the logical choice to take care of the Aston Martins. He made six shooting brakes using the longer base of the DB6. The design of the rear was adapted to the truncations that were characteristic of this model. Another coachmaker did the same transformation: FLM (Panelcraft) Ltd, a workshop opened in Battersea by some former employees of the bodywork maker James Young, H. S. Fry, Robert Lee and W. McNally. The three DB6 shooting brakes made by FLM are distinguished by the original and not entirely successful design of the side glazing.

The style inflicted on the DB6 by the bodywork maker FLM Panelcraft is debatable.

**Above left:** The Volante version of the DB6 had the benefit of four comfortable seats but also had to accept a truncated rear end. **Above right:** The DB6 Mark II had wider wheel rims that required beading around the wheel arches.

# CHANGE OF COURSE WITH THE DB6

Announced at the London Motor Show in 1965, the DB6 was a logical development of the DB5, but there were numerous changes relative to its predecessor, both in form and in spirit. The wheelbase was increased from 249 to 258 cm, which, together with a new design of the passenger compartment, allowed for more comfortable rear passenger seats to the detriment of the car's aesthetics. This development was not unique to the DB6—most grand touring cars were doing the same thing. In most similar cases, when two-seater coupés were transformed into 2+2s or 4-seaters, the change completely altered the style. The Jaguar E-Type suffered when it became a '2+2', as did the Mercedes-Benz SLC created out of the SL. At the front, the bumpers of the DB6 were now in two halves and an air intake was placed below them for the oil radiator. The rear included fashionable truncations surmounted by a spoiler. The capacity of the luggage compartment was enhanced more than aerodynamics.

The power train did not change, with the engine still providing 266 hp and a choice between a five-speed manual gearbox (ZF) or automatic transmission (Borg Warner). The Vantage option was maintained for more sporty drivers: it now managed 325 hp at 5,750 rpm. Markedly more civilised than its predecessors, the DB6 had power steering. This was a useful innovation given the substantial weight gain of this knowingly understeering car. In October 1966, the Volante convertible turned into the DB6 Volante and thus became more homogeneous with the DB6 Saloon by adopting its long chassis and truncated rear. The loss in aesthetic terms was a gain in habitability. A second series of the DB6 (Mark II) was announced in August 1969. The wheel arches were slightly enlarged to accommodate larger wheels.

Its career came to an end in July 1969. The total production tally was as follows: 1,327 DB6 saloons, nine of which were converted into shooting brakes, three by Harold Radford, three by FLN Panelcraft in a more convoluted style; 140 DB6 Volantes, of which twenty-nine in the Vantage option with automatic transmission.

DBSC is one of the last projects developed by Touring before the company closed its doors.

# THE DBSC: A MISSED OPPORTUNITY (1966)

At the Paris Car Show, which took place 6–16 October 1966 at Porte de Versailles, Aston Martin exhibited a new car that marked a break with the developments that had taken place between the DB4 and the DB6, Over successive generations, the coupé had become more respectable and had shed its sporty reputation as it had gained in comfort. With the DBSC, Aston Martin returned to the values that had underpinned the success of the DB4 and the DB5. The new car had a short wheelbase and made a deliberate decision to limit habitability to two seats.

The DBSC was developed in close cooperation with Touring. It had a more incisive style than the DB5: the edges were sharpened, the flanks stretched and traversed by a rib and the rear neatly truncated and punctuated by two large circular lights.

Unfortunately, Touring had run into difficulties. They were put under state administration in 1963, and underwent a first wave of redundancies. Production finally came to an end on 31 January 1967, and their factory in Milan was taken over by an industrial chemical group.

Given these circumstances, Aston Martin stopped production of the DBSC, of which two prototypes were built (266-1/R and 2/L).

# THE LOLA-ASTON MARTIN
# T70 MARK III GT

At the Racing Car Show in London in January 1967, Lola exhibited the T70 Mark III GT, a closed version of the model entered for the Can-Am Challenge. The version destined for private ecuries was sold with a Chevrolet engine, while the two cars officially adopted by Team Surtees (SL73/101 and 121) were equipped with an Aston Martin engine. This was the V8 5-litre DP218, which prefigured the mechanics of the future DB V8. Presented in a dark-green livery, the T70 Mark III GT was a superb car, but its performances on the track, at the Nüburgring and at Le Mans, were disappointing.

The superb Lola-Aston Martin T70 Mark III no. SL73/101 at the weigh-in on the eve of the Le Mans 24 Hours in 1967.

# THE DB5 IN *GOLDFINGER*

The fame of the DB5 is due to one rather famous client, the secret agent 007. In the original book by Ian Fleming, Mr Bond—James Bond—drove a DB Mark III, but when *Goldfinger* was filmed in 1965, directed by Guy Hamilton, they preferred the more up-to-date DB5.

James Bond's DB5 was kitted out with a number of accessories that do not appear in the Aston Martin catalogue: Browning rifles hidden under the bumpers, a bullet-proof windscreen, a telescopic bullet-proof screen that came out of the rear boot, interchangeable number plates, an ejector seat in case of an unwelcome passenger, retractable wheel nuts to lacerate a neighbour's tyres and devices for spreading oil or nails on the road to discourage over-insistent pursuers.

Four separate cars were prepared for the film. The car that was fitted out for the special effects was returned to Aston Martin after the filming to be stripped of its paraphernalia. Since this car was very heavy, the filmmakers used a standard model (chassis no. 1486/R) when shooting the normal scenes. Two other DB5s were made to promote the film and for the filming of *Thunderball* (nos. 2008/R and 2017/R). The first was bequeathed to the Smoky Mountain Car Museum in Tennessee; the second became part of the collection at Cars of the Stars in Keswick in the north of England.

**Left:** The fame of the DB5 is inseparable from the personality of Sean Connery. **Above:** The DB5 used in *Goldfinger*, exhibited on the Aston Martin stand at the Paris Car Show in 1965.

A new era begins with the DBS designed by William Towns.

# DBS: A NEW ERA

With the coming of the DBS, Aston Martin began to diversify. This coupé added an element of sportiness and modernity to the DB6.

At the end of the 1960s, Britain was still an island. The natives remained wary of the idea of connecting themselves to the continent via a tunnel. Besides, who on earth would want to join this so-called Community that some Europeans had had the impudence to found? Until the Channel Tunnel opened in 1994, the British resisted all physical contact with the rest of the world. They did nothing like anyone else—neither cars, nor cream cakes nor detective novels. British cars weren't obsolete, they were timeless. Apart from the double-decker Routemaster buses and the Austin black cabs, what was to be seen on the streets of Canterbury or Edinburgh? Vehicles of enormous charm that those eaters of snails and frog's legs across the Channel neither understood nor deserved. It would be inappropriate to talk about modernism and English industry in the same breath. The excesses of a modernity that fed on functionalism and plastic cut little ice in the homeland of Bentley and other institutions that had carved their conservatism in burr walnut.

On the first series of the DBS the side panels were pierced with vents.

# THE DBS SALOON:
# THE NEGLECTED LINK (1967–1973)

At the end of the 1960s, Aston Martin thought about enlarging its range and supplementing the DB6 with a more sporty model. Touring were once again consulted and they presented the results of their research in October 1966 in the form of the DBSC (see Chapter 2). But rumours concerning the sustainability of Touring as a going concern were becoming increasingly alarming, and the Aston Martin management opted for a 'Plan B' instead. They had on file a counter-proposition submitted by William Towns based on simple lines, sufficiently sharpened to introduce a note of modernity.

The DBS was built on a chassis that followed the schema of the DB6 but was wider and longer. The engine was placed further down to lower the centre of gravity, and a new de Dion type rear axle was used. As for the engine, the capacity remained unchanged at 282 hp at 5,500 rpm. From the start, Aston Martin offered a Vantage option that was noticeably more vigorous: fed by three Weber 45DCOE carburettors, this variant generated 325 hp, like the DB6 Vantage engine. Aston Martin also offered a fuel injection system supplied by AE Brico. Between 1967 and 1972, 1,193 DBS six-cylinders were produced.

In May 1972, David Brown's initials disappeared as soon as he retired from the business. A whole symbol. The DBS continued to exist only in its most powerful version and became simply the 'Vantage'. Its front end was modernised: the large grille that spanned its whole width and included the four headlights was replaced by a smaller, nicely sculpted radiator grille, with the headlights encased in dedicated fittings.

The days of the six-cylinders were numbered: production of the Vantage ceased after little more than a year of service in August 1973; only seventy were made.

# WILLIAM TOWNS: HEAD OF SCHOOL

British design had a duty to maintain certain standards. The colleges were there to ensure this. The ancient College of Design and the Birmingham College of Art and Design both had chairs dedicated to the teaching of design.

In 1969, the highly respected Royal College of Art in London added to its course a programme dedicated to modes of transport, a first in Europe. In this arena British industry had several remarkable and eminently qualified individuals.

At Vauxhall, the man in charge of the design studio, David Jones, had studied under Henry Moore at the Royal College of Art. At British Leyland, Harris Mann, an engineer by training, learned about design from Raymond Loewy. At Rover, David Bache had played a major role in modernising their style by completing the study for the first Range Rover, which opened the way for all the SUVs of the future.

One of the UK's most original talents was William Towns. Born in 1936, he started out working for Rootes in 1954, then designed the memorable turbine Rover-BRM in 1965 before founding the Interstyl studio based in Moreton-on-Marsh in Gloucestershire. Apart from his work for Aston Martin, William Towns conceived a number of visionary projects such as the run-around Minissima (1973) and the frugal Hustler (1978). Towns would die of cancer in 1993 at the age of forty-seven.

**Top left:** The double-decker Routemaster bus, manufactured by AEC, is one of the clichés associated with Great Britain. **Top middle:** The clever Bond Bug created by Tom Karen. **Top right:** At the opposite end of the scale from the DBS, William Towns designed the Minissima for British Leyland. **Above left:** In 1965, William Towns designed the turbine prototype of the Rover-BRM. **Above right:** The Vauxhall XVR was characterised by a formidable mastery of volume.

# A FOUR-DOOR DBS

In the autumn of 1969, David Brown had a four-door saloon made for himself, based on a DBS (chassis MP230/1). It retained the general silhouette of the coupé and particularly the receding, profiled rear which contributes a great deal to the look of the car. Five years later a similar car was put into production.

**Top:** The DBS specially remodelled (no. MP230/1) as a saloon for David Brown. **Above:** This DBS no. 5636/R, issued in May 1970, was disguised as a DBS V8 for the television series *The Persuaders*, starring Roger Moore and Tony Curtis.

The DBS V8 features GKN light alloy wheels.

# FROM THE DBS V8
# TO THE V8 (1969–1989)

The DBS V8, which appeared in September 1969, inaugurated the new eight-cylinder engine developed by the engineer Tadek Marek. The general contours hadn't changed, but the front cradle had been fitted out to accommodate the heavier and bulkier engine. There was a voluminous trim supporting the 5.3-litre Bosch injection V8, whose power was estimated at about 310/320 hp, but Aston Martin—like Rolls-Royce—no longer disclosed this data. The spoked wheels could not handle the extra power, so they were replaced by light alloy wheels supplied by GKN. Mass production of the DBS V8 began in April 1970. Two years later, in April 1972, the DBS V8 became simply the 'Aston Martin V8', thereby erasing any reference to David Brown. It was distinguished by its more harmonious front, the same as that of the Vantage six-cylinder.

In 1970, the US administration introduced the Clean Air Act designed to reduce atmospheric pollution. The Environmental Protection Agency (EPA) imposed a reduction in emissions of sulphur dioxide and carbon monoxide, and all the constructors were forced to apply this stipulation. However, the engineers at Aston Martin had difficulty bringing their Bosch injection engine into line with the new American regulations. Also, from July 1973, carburettors were reintroduced under the bonnet of the V8, which, to cover them, had to be equipped with a more substantial boss. The power fell from 310 hp to around 280 hp.

Aston Martin Lagonda was hit hard by the economic crisis of 1973. The firm was on the brink of going under and suspended production between December 1974 and March 1976. Only the after-sales division remained open during these long months. Symbolically, the relaunch was announced in October 1976 at the Motor Show, which took place for the final time at Earl's Court in London before migrating to Birmingham. Aston Martin were hoping to make a splash with the iconoclastic Lagonda with its extravagant lines.

# THE ASTON MARTIN LAGONDA

The Aston Martin Lagonda, produced in dribs and drabs from 1974 to 1976.

At the London Motor Show in 1974, Aston Martin exhibited a judicious four-door variant of the V8. It retained the general contours of the DBS no. MP240/1 made for David Brown. Only the front had been redesigned by integrating a radiator grille meant to illustrate the Lagonda brand, for this model was the first to combine the names of the two former brands: Aston Martin Lagonda. Only seven of these cars were produced between August 1974 and May 1976.

# BULLDOG: THE CONCEPT CAR (1980)

William Towns was asked to design the Bulldog (Project DPK901), which was meant to illustrate the future of Aston Martin by adopting an architecture organised around a central engine, a design synonymous with modernity. The development was led by Mike Loasby, who would later join De Lorean to work on a product with the same theme. The 5,340 cc V8 engine had two turbo-compressors and it enabled the Bulldog to reach speeds of more than 300 km/h. After being presented to the press on 27 March 1980 at the Bell Hotel, Aston Clinton, the concept car was sent to the United States to make its public debut in April at the Los Angeles Auto Expo.

The Bulldog was treated in an angular style around a pyramidal volume.

In May 1972, the DBS V8 became the AM V8 and received a new front end. Additional headlamps were optional.

For the 1979 vintage, Aston Martin made modifications to the V8 which were codenamed 'Oscar India', the initials standing for 'October introduction'. On this fourth series, the rear was finished off with a discreet spoiler, the hood boss no longer contained an air intake, the dashboard was once again made of wood, and automatic transmission—a three-speed Torqueflite provided by Chrysler—was chosen by most customers in preference to the five-speed ZF manual transmission.

In 1980, the engine evolved from the V540 type to the modified V580 in terms of its distribution and cylinder heads. From 1983, the GKN wheels were replaced by BBS types.

The final evolution to the V8 Saloon, the fifth series, came in January 1986 with the introduction of a Weber electronic injection system, which removed the need for any boss on the bonnet. The rims were furnished by a succession of suppliers, ending with Ronal.

The production tally for the V8, over the span of twenty years, comes to the following:

+ DBS V8, with injection engine: 404 produced between September 1969 and May 1972;

+ V8 Series 2, with injection engine: 288 produced between April 1972 and July 1973;

+ V8 Series 3, with carburettors: 967 produced between July 1973 and September 1978;

+ V8 Series 4, 'Oscar India', with carburettors: 293 (sixty-four of them left-hand drive) produced between October 1978 and January 1986;

+ V8 Series 5, with V585 injection engine: sixty-one produced between January 1986 and October 1989.

The V8 Vantage in its original form in January 1977.

## THE DBS V8 AS SEEN BY OGLE

This Sotheby Special, designed by Tom Karen, was one of only three ever produced.

A Czech by birth, Tom Karen headed up one of the most reputable independent design studios in Britain after 1962, when its founder, David Ogle, died in an accident. The studio worked across many industrial sectors and had some brilliant hits such as the Reliant Scimitar GTE, a coupé cum estate car released in October 1968, and especially the ingenious cuneiform three-wheeler Bond Bug, launched in 1970. Ogle's company was both a design agency that worked on projects for constructors and a production workshop for limited series. Ogle also made concept cars. In Montreal, in January 1972, then in Geneva in March, we find a coupé based on the DBS V8 that bears the name of its sponsor, a cigarette manufacturer: Sotheby Special. Only three of this strange coupé designed by Tom Karen were ever made.

74

**Above:** If the client so desired, the passenger space of the V8 Vantage could be covered in leather. **Following pages:** On the V8 Vantage, on Series II as well as all the others, the radiator grille was obscured.

## The V8 Vantage: A Supercar According to Aston Martin (1977–1989)

The V8 Vantage appeared in February 1977. It was superlative on every score: attitude, performance and price. Everything was outsized on this monster of a car: valves, Weber 48IDF carburettors, power increased to 375 hp, 255/60VR15 tyres, reinforced chassis, hardened suspension and adjustable Koni shock absorbers. Stylistically too it spoke excess, with its large boss on the bonnet, the aerodynamic deflector almost skimming the tarmac and the impressive spoiler attached to the boot. The radiator grille was obscured by a plate integrating two large Cibié headlamps.

From October 1978, the V8 Vantage benefitted from improvements listed under the codename 'Oscar India': the rear spoiler was integrated and the dashboard was upholstered in leather. When the Saloon V8 readopted injection, with a Weber/Marelli system, in January 1986, the Vantage, listed under the code V580X, did not follow suit and kept faith with its four dual-body carburettors. The V8 remained a rare beast: only a little over 300 cars were produced, divided up as follows:

+ V8 Vantage Series 1, with V540 engine: thirty-nine produced between February 1977 and September 1978;

+ V8 Vantage Series 2, 'Oscar India': forty-four with V540 engine produced between October 1978 and March 1980, ninety-four with V580X engine after 1980;

+ V8 Vantage X-Pack, with V580X engine: 137 produced between October 1986 and December 1989.

Presentation of the V8 Volante at the Birmingham Motor Show in October 1978.

# The Return of the Volante (1978–1989)

With the demise of the DB6, Aston Martin no longer offered a convertible for sale. Apart from a few artisanal adaptations, such as those of Paul Banham and Specialised Engineering Ltd, the DBS had never appeared in an official convertible version. It wasn't until June 1978 that the V8 Volante came along. With it, walnut grain was once more a feature of dashboards. The Volante was equipped with an electrically operated, lined hood, which was developed by the engineer who had designed the canvas roof of the Rolls-Royce Corniche.

The first series was driven by a carburettor engine close to 305 hp. But matching this to American regulations proved tricky, so the engineers opted to revert to electronic injection. In January 1986, the adoption of the Weber power system boosted the power to 315 hp. Aston Martin sold 216 of these cars prior to 1989.

In October 1986, at the Birmingham Motor Show, Aston Martin launched the V8 Vantage Volante, which had an even more aggressive bodywork than the coupé version. It of course retained the imposing spoiler under the front bumper and the spoiler on the boot, but as a bonus had thick skirts at the bottom of the body and enlarged wheel arches. More than a third of the V8 Volante Vantages produced between October 1986 and December 1989 were destined for the American market: they are equipped with the 580X carburettor pack providing more than 400 hp.

In 1988, Aston Martin produced twenty-seven V8 Volantes which they baptised PoW, in honour of the Prince of Wales, who had asked for a number of modifications to his own car. Not fully appreciating the ostentatious quality of the V8 Vantage, he asked them to remove the spoiler, replace the thick side skirts with thinner units made of polished stainless steel and soften the arc of the wheel arches to receive 16-inch Ronal wheels.

The V8 Volante had all the credentials to become a star of the auction houses—a limited edition with a muscular aesthetic:

- The V8 Volante, with carburettors: 439, 282 of them left-hand drive, produced between June 1978 and January 1985;

- The V8 Volante, with injection engine: 166, seventy-eight of them with the X-Pack, produced between January 1986 and December 1989;

- The V8 Vantage Volante: 167, fifty-eight of them with the V580X engine, produced between October 1986 and December 1989.

**Top:** With its side skirts, rimmed wheel arches and spoiler, the V8 Volante Vantage plays the sporty card. **Above:** The boss on the bonnet of this 1981 model is due to the inclusion of carburettors.

The profile of the Lagonda—here a Series II from 1981—is somewhat caricatural with its exaggerated overhang.

## The Metamorphoses of Aston Martin Lagonda (1972–1981)

Over the course of the DBS's long career, in its various versions, which lasted from 1967 to 1989, the company underwent some profound changes. It all began in the wake of the first oil crisis. On 6 October 1973, in Riyadh, the members of OPEC (Organization of the Petroleum Exporting Countries) decided to reduce their fuel deliveries until the rights of the Palestinians were restored. The price of oil immediately rocketed by 68 percent and unleashed an economic crisis which entailed traffic and speed restrictions. The geopolitical dimension of the oil crisis alerted the world to the precarious nature of energy sources and forced industry to reduce its fuel consumption. This new consciousness was accompanied by the breakthrough of green parties in Germany and France.

In the United States, regulations on emissions were tightened. The backlash against manufacturers of high-performance cars was not far behind.

On 16 February 1972, Aston Martin Lagonda was placed under the control of Company Developments, a group of businessmen based in Birmingham and directed by William Willson. David Brown had a seat on the board of directors. The projects in progress, submitted by Trevor Fiore in October 1971, were brought into question: a modular coupé with a transaxle architecture and a berlinetta with a BRM central engine. The new management did not succeed in turning things around, and the company went bust for the first time in December 1974.

Company Developments decided to put Aston Martin Lagonda up for sale, and it was acquired in June 1975 by the North American industrialists Peter Sprague and George Minden, in partnership with Jeremy Turner, a London businessman, who were joined by Alan Curtis and George Flather. The negotiations were led by Peter Sprague, aged thirty-five, a Harvard graduate and a businessman with a reputation for saving companies in difficulty, like National Semiconductor, a poultry farm and a furniture manufacturer. George Minden, a luxury car seller in Toronto and hotel owner, would concentrate on building up sales in America. Jeremy Turner, twenty-nine, a communications expert who worked in the world of luxury cars, yachts and business aviation, would be responsible for product development.

# THE MANAGEMENT OF VICTOR GAUNTLETT (1981–1987)

Barely out the other side of the oil crisis, the world economy took another hit when the Middle East once more erupted in flames with the war between Iran and Iraq in September 1980. The price of a barrel of oil went from $13 to $50, which brought new coercive measures in its wake.

In January 1981, Aston Martin Lagonda changed hands again. Two companies took control of it: Pace Petroleum, a petroleum distribution company presided over by Victor Gauntlett, and CH Industrials, a nationalised company, directed by Tim Hearley, which made components for the car industry. Gauntlett had already sat on the board of AML and had held a 10 percent stake in the company since May 1980.

In July 1983, Automotive Investments Inc. (AII) bought the shares held by Pace Petroleum and thus held 55 percent of the shares of Aston Martin Lagonda; CH Industrials retained the rest. Victor Gauntlett remained in post as president and managing director. AII, a US importer of Aston Martins, was led by Peter Livanos, who came from a family of ship owners.

In February 1984, CH Industrials in turn sold its shares to Automotive Investments Inc., which thus ended up owning 100 percent of Aston Martin Lagonda for eight months. In October 1984, the shares were once more parcelled out, with 75 percent for Peter Livanos and 25 percent for Victor Gauntlett.

## THE CRAZY LAGONDA (1976–1987)

The fourth series of the Lagonda had a bodywork with lines that were less sharp than on the second and third series. This car (no. 13601) dates from 1989.

The reconstruction plan began to take shape with the launch of the Aston Martin Lagonda at the London Motor Show in 1976. This car based on the V8 Saloon was intended to make a statement after the recent years of jeopardy. William Towns came up with a radical style, extremely sharp, with exaggerated proportions. In total, only 645 of these cars were produced of Series II and III of this controversial model. In March 1987, Series IV featured a redesigned body with softened surfaces and blunted corners. Aston Martin manufactured only ninety-eight of this series, which was terminated in January 1980.

The Nimrod NRA/C2 no. 001 at its presentation in 1981.

# PRIVATE INITIATIVES IN ENDURANCE RACING (1981–1985)

Aston Martin Lagonda was receptive to supporting private initiatives which used their machines. They had an association with Nimrod Racing Automobiles, created by Robin Hamilton, an Aston Martin distributor in Staffordshire. Nimrod was entering the endurance world championship with the NRA/C2, developed by Lola Cars and using an engine made by Aston Martin Tickford Ltd, a 5.3-litre V8. Tested in 1981, the car made its debut at Silverstone in May 1982. At the Le Mans 24 Hours, the Nimrod, driven by Ray Mallock, Simon Phillips and Mike Salmon, finished seventh.

For the 1983 championship, the prototype that raced under the colours of Viscount Downe with Pace Petroleum (chassis 004) was modified by Ray Mallock. A fifth chassis (no. 005) was used for the first time at the Daytona 24 Hours in 1984. Over three years of racing, the Nimrod NRA/C2 and C2B rarely shone and proved unreliable.

In 1983, another team developed a prototype driven by an Aston Martin engine. Emka Racing, whose particular claim to fame was it was run by Steve O'Rourke, who became manager of Pink Floyd after the death of Syd Barrett. After having run different types of car (Ferrari, BMW), he became a constructor in 1983. The Emka C83/1, built by Michael Cane Racing, was designed by Len Bailey, who had worked for Ford, Alan Mann and Frank Williams. In 1985, it came in eleventh at the Le Mans 24 Hours, its best result.

The third constructor to choose the Aston Martin V8 was Cheetah Automobiles, a workshop created in 1964 by Chuck Graemiger in Lausanne. Their prototype G604 competed in a number of trials in 1984 and 1985, but without success.

# FORD ENTERS THE SCENE (1987)

Victor Gauntlett did not manage to bring his plans to fruition. He had wanted to expand his range to attract new clients. He had envisaged acquiring the rights to manufacture the Magnum, a competitor of the Range Rover created by the Italian car maker Rayton Fissore. "We should not simply be present in the sports car market. We need to be, no doubt, but wouldn't it be wonderful to have a great variety of vehicles with a traditional Aston, a vehicle such as a Magnum and a more accessible sporty Aston?" Gauntlett's only mistake was to be right too soon: the small Aston would arrive in 2005 and the first SUV in 2019!

In September 1987, Ford Motor Company acquired a 75 percent stake in the company, with Gauntlett and the Livanos family splitting the other 25 percent, Gauntlett would stay firmly in place as president. He didn't retire until September 1991, making way for Walter Hayes, who had formerly been vice president of Ford Europe.

## THE ASTON MARTIN AMR1

In 1988, Victor Gauntlett decided to invest personally in a new sporting programme via Proteus Technology Protech. The Scottish ecurie was commissioned to develop and manage the AMR1 project with Ray Mallock as technical director and Max Boxstrom as chief engineer. The chassis was constructed by Courtaulds and the engine (V8, 6 litres, 650 hp) put together by Callaway. Five AMR1 chassis were built in 1989. In the face of fierce opposition from Sauber, Jaguar, Porsche and Nissan, the Aston Martin AMR1s struggled. Their best result of the year—sixth place for the pair David Leslie and Brian Redman—was recorded at Brands Hatch.

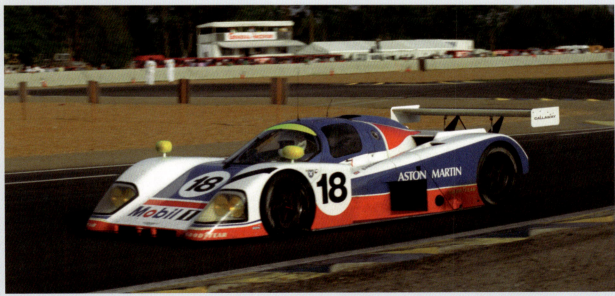

The AMR1 driven by Costas Los, Brian Redman and Michael Roe, which came in eleventh at the Le Mans 24 Hours in 1989.

The V8 Vantage line culminated in 1996 with the V600 version.

# VIRAGE: A DECISIVE TURNING POINT

The takeover of Aston Martin by Ford in 1987 did not have an immediate impact on the product range. The Virage, the latest version of the DBS, was developed without any interference from the American group.

It was time to turn the page on the V8, née DBS. Two decades is a long time in the world of specialist cars, a market that gorged on novelty, innovation and obsolescence. In a sense, the DP 2034 project was launched by Victor Gauntlett in 1986 before Ford had really picked up the reins at Aston Martin. This newcomer had to be an extension of the previous models, keep their classic architecture and preserve as many of their components as possible. The designers also had to take into account the heavier production load. In terms of style, the specifications advocated a more consensual approach, able to attract a customer base beyond the usual die-hard fans of the brand.

**Above:** The first prototype of the DP2034 project was improvised from a truncated Lagonda. **Above right:** The preliminary sketches made by John Hefferman for the future Virage.

# THE DUO JOHN HEFFERMAN
# AND KEN GREENLEY

In the 1980s, John Heffermean and Ken Greenley formed a very prolific creative partnership. Apart from their one-off contracts, the two designers taught at the Royal College of Art, where Greenley held a chair in transport design. They came to notice in the car world during the 1980s with their design for the Panther Solo, a berlinetta with a central engine, and the Bentley Project 90, which prefigured the Continental R. In 1994, Ken Greenley was guilty of designing the SsangYong Rodius, considered to be one of the ugliest cars ever designed!

John Hefferman and Ken Greenley gained their reputation by creating the Project 90 for Bentley in 1985.

The Virage as it looked in October 1988.

# THE VIRAGE INAUGURATES
# A NEW LINE (1988–1996)

The first prototype was elaborated in 1987 from a Lagonda saloon, which was shortened and transformed into a two-door coupé, which gave it an odd appearance. While this strange mule of a car was undergoing tests, a style study took place, setting five designers in competition with each other, among them William Towns, the creator of the DBS and the Lagonda, as well as Richard Oakes, creator of the Nova, a berlinetta sold in kit form, and the duo John Hefferman and Ken Greenley.

At the end of the day, the theme that was chosen was that of the latter two. Their styling exuded an undeniable sense of power, combining massive volume, a high body, a short wheelbase and a flattened interior, but it was not unanimous. The whole lacked finesse, and the use of several accessories from mass-market cars was criticised: headlights borrowed from the Audi 200, rear lights from the Volkswagen Sirocco and indicator lights from the Porsche 911.

For the first time at Aston Martin, aerodynamics were taken into account on a passenger car. The 1:4 scale model was subjected to the MIRA wind tunnel test, where it was given a drag coefficient (Cx) of 0.35. The Motor Industry Research Association (MIRA) in Warwickshire offered a number of facilities to constructors to help them develop their products.

**Above left:** The driving console of the Virage. **Above right:** The V8 engine of the Virage had four valves per cylinder.

In the interior of the Virage everything was state of the art. The dials retained an analogue display, but an on-board computer and a digital watch appeared for the first time. A new material, Alcantara, a sort of synthetic suede, was used to cover the dashboard. Adjustable heated seats showed the attention paid to improving comfort. In the same spirit, the capacity of the boot was expanded, suggesting the car was to be used for long trips.

As for the mechanics, there were other noticeable signs of progress. The V8, which now ran off lead-free petrol, produced 330 hp: it had cylinder heads with four valves per cylinder which had been developed in collaboration with Callaway Engineering, a firm based in Connecticut.

The Virage was unveiled on 18 October 1988 at the Motor Show in Birmingham, where two pre-series models were displayed: one silver grey (DP2034/3), the other dark green (DP2034/4).

## The Virage Volante (1990–1996)

September 1990 marked the appearance of the Volante version of the Virage developed in cooperation with the engineering consulting firm Hawtal Whiting. Unlike the former V8 Volante, this convertible Virage was at first strictly limited to two seats. In the production models that became available a few months later, the Volante had adopted the 2+2 configuration of its predecessor. The hood was hydraulically operated. Only 233 of this type were produced, 120 with left-hand drive for the overseas market. The vast majority of the cars were driven by a 330 hp engine connected to a Torqueflite automatic gearbox. Only twenty-seven cars were fitted with the five-speed manual gearbox. The last ten Volante convertibles enjoyed an enhanced 349 hp of power.

Some Volantes were later converted to the 6.3-litre engine and/or wider frame. All these additions collectively create confusion as to the degree of transformation!

In 1995, to mark the sixtieth anniversary of the first meeting of the Aston Martin Owner's Club (AMOC), the jeweller Cartier collaborated with Aston Martin to sell a Volante (no. 60500) adorned with diamonds, rubies and emeralds worth $1.25 million.

**Top:** The Diamond Jubilee Volante had a wide body but kept the 5.3-litre engine. **Above:** Despite certain concessions to modernity, the interior of the Virage Volante remained thoroughly traditional.

The Virage Volante went on the market in January 1992 with air outlets on the front wings.

## The Return of the V8 Vantage (1992–1999)

The V8 Vantage label turns up again and again in the history of Aston Martin to designate very dissimilar, unrelated models that have no continuity with each other.

In Birmingham in October 1992, the V8 Vantage based on the Virage (code DP2055) was unveiled in the form of a prototype. Compared to the Virage, the front of the V8 Vantage was much softer. There were new optics consisting of two sets of three square projectors placed under a globe, air outlets on the front fenders and front and rear shields. Only the roof and the doors had been preserved from the Virage.

Thanks to two Eaton turbocompressors, the 5.3-litre engine generated 550 hp to begin with, and by the end of 1996 the more muscular V600 version managed 600 hp at 6,500 rpm. This shock treatment was applied to twenty-four engines, while there were 239 cars produced in total between 1992 and 1999.

# THE VIRAGE GT LIGHTWEIGHT (1991)

In 1991, a Virage (chassis 10558/L) was sent to the German distributor Car & Driver in Hamburg with the blessing of Aston Martin. Equipped with a 6.3-litre engine, the car was lightened by about 250 kg thanks to the use of Alcantara rather than wood on the dashboard and on-board panels and the removal of the rear seats. The plan was to produce twenty-five of these lighter cars, but the operation proved too expensive (about 500,000 DM), and this remained the only car of its type.

**Top:** This unique Virage GT Lightweight was made for Aston Martin's German distributor. **Above:** These new optics, consisting of three square-shaped headlights, were originally confined to the V8 Vantage, but later became standard across all the models from 1996.

# THE 6.3-LITRE VERSION (1992)

In January 1992, a new variant was announced. It had been developed by Tickford Engineering and offered by the Customer Service Division. The capacity had increased to 6.3 litres (6,347 cc), and the power to 465 hp thanks to a Weber Alpha injection system. Subsequently, the efficiency was increased to 500 hp at 6,000 rpm thanks to special camshafts; the suspension was then modified accordingly. The bodywork of the 6.3 litre was embellished with a spoiler on the boot, side air outlets and enlarged wheel arches to accommodate OZ wheels with 285/45 tyres. This conversion, costing more than £60,000, would be applied to twenty-four cars only. At Birmingham in 1992 there was a further escalation, with a variant fitted with two turbocompressors which could attain 550 hp.

A large engine increased to 6.3 litres and a hypertrophied bodywork go hand in hand in this extreme version of the Vantage V8 in 1992.

# THE LIMITED EDITION COUPÉ (1994)

The Limited Edition special series launched in October 1994 to boost the appeal of the V8 Vantage.

The arrival of the DB7 had distracted the buyers of the Virage. In order to attract customers back to the models with V8 engines, it was necessary to make them more attractive with some special added benefits. It was with this in mind that the Aston Martin Limited Edition Coupé was presented at Birmingham in October 1994 with a price tag of £137,500. The nine cars produced (nos. 50411 to 50419) are recognisable by their metallic dark-green livery and radiator grille with its V-shaped grid. Thanks to modified electronic controls, the V8 5.3-litre engine generated 349 hp and could be combined with either a manual or an automatic gearbox.

In March 1996, the Virage was renamed the V8 Coupé and adopted the same front end as the V8 Vantage.

# A SECOND GENERATION (1996–2000)

The Virage had already upgraded its current name to the banal 'V8 Coupé' in 1994. The new label was ratified in March 1996 when the restructured range was announced at the Geneva Car Show. It consisted of the V8 Coupé, the V8 Volante and the V8 Vantage.

The V8 Coupé was driven by a 5.3-litre engine producing 249 hp and connected to a four-speed automatic gearbox. It now had the same physiognomy as the V8 Vantage with its softer features, but without its enlarged wheel arches. Over the course of its life, the V8 Coupé (101 produced in total) would trade in its Citroën mirrors for some rather less ordinary parts supplied by Jaguar.

The V8 Vantage didn't undergo these changes, since it had the new front end with six headlights from its inception in 1992.

In March 1996, the Volante was brought into line with the V8 Coupé and acquired the same rounded front. In addition, from October 1997, Aston Martin produced a small series (sixty-three units) with an extended wheelbase to make the car roomier and more comfortable for four people. The majority of these rather expensive cars (£169,500) were earmarked for export across the Atlantic.

# THE WORKS SERVICE

One of the V8 Sportsman cars (no. 79007) made in 1996 by the Works Service.

Formerly called the 'Customer Service Division', the department that came to be known as the Works Service took care of special orders. Some remained confidential, others were revealed officially. Thus, in March, Aston Martin gave out information about two versions of the Virage fitted with four doors and built on an extended wheelbase: a saloon and a Vacances shooting brake. Two brothers in Switzerland ordered two identical Sportsman shooting brakes based on the V8 Coupé (nos. 79007 and 79008). Started in July 1996, the two made-over cars, painted in the famous Racing Green, were completed in December 1997. One of them was auctioned by Bonhams in Newport Pagnell for £375,856 in 2017. Most of the cars created by the Works Service remained a secret because many of them were ordered by the Sultan of Brunei, His Majesty Hassanal Bolkiah Mu'izzadin Waddaulah, a super-rich car collector and acquirer of several specially customised vehicles. The Sultan's garages were filled with road versions of competition cars, extrapolations of berlinettas in the form of saloons, estates or SUVs, and special types of bodywork. He had each new creation made in a small series of three, to have spares to give as gifts to family members or his most loyal collaborators. Aston Martin fashioned saloons, estates and berlinettas out of the V8 Coupé for this loyal customer; some of them were subcontracted to Pininfarina.

In 1994, Aston Martin officially announced these two Virages developed by the Works Service, the saloon and Vacances shooting brake.

Covered radiator grille, ovoid air outlets on the wings and bonnet indented with two notches made the V8 Vantage Le Mans identifiable.

## Climax with the V8 Vantage at Le Mans (1999–2000)

At the Geneva Car Show in March 1999, Aston Martin celebrated the fortieth anniversary of its victory in the Le Mans 24 Hours.

Mechanically speaking, the V8 Vantage Le Mans offered the same benefits as the V8 Vantage in its V550 and V600 versions. For the occasion, the radiator grille was obstructed, covered with a painted plate in which two circular holes had been cut out. The bonnet had an opening that helped to hold the front to the ground. The air outlets on the wings had the ovoid shape of those of its predecessor DBR1-300. Only fourteen V8 Vantage Le Mans would be produced between March 1999 and October 2000.

The DB7 Vantage differs from the original DB7 by its large projectors embedded in the shield.

# DB7: A CHANGE OF DIRECTION

Although Ford didn't interfere with plans for the Virage, it was the American parent company that orchestrated the design of the DB7, which was destined for a new clientele as far as Aston Martin was concerned.

A lot of things changed for Aston Martin at the beginning of the 1990s. David Brown, who had remained honorary life president of Aston Martin Lagonda, passed away on 3 September 1993 at the age of eighty-nine. In February 1994, Walter Hayes, who had symbolised the arrival of Ford at Newport Pagnell, was replaced by John Oldfield as president of the company. Both were mainstays of the Ford Motor Company, the ultra-loyalists. John Oldfield began working there at the age of twenty-one!

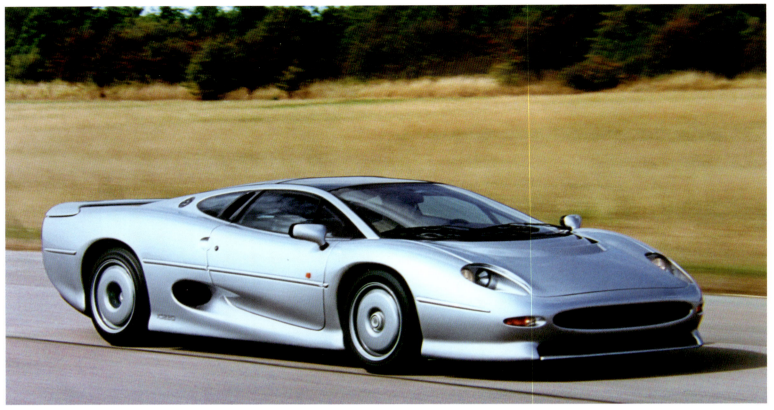

The Aston Martin DB7 would take the place of the Jaguar XJ 220 in the factory at Bloxham.

# A NEW DIMENSION

The car industry at this time was undergoing widespread changes of ownership. There were multiple mergers and takeovers, marriages and divorces. Fiat Auto bought a 49 percent stake in Maserati and took control of the company in May 1993. The British Leyland Motor Corporation, which had accumulated eleven other brands (Austin, Austin-Healey, Daimler, Jaguar, MG, Morris, Riley, Rover, Triumph, Vanden Plas and Wolseley), focused its portfolio to concentrate on Austin Rover in 1982 and then uniquely Rover in 1986. Bought by British Aerospace in 1988, taken over by BMW in February 1994, Rover was finally acquired by Phoenix Venture Holdings in May 2000. Land Rover, also acquired by BMW, would be sold to Ford in March 2000 and later to the Indian group Tata. No one was spared these manoeuvrings: Lamborghini came under the wing of Chrysler between April 1987 and January 1994. After the fall of the Berlin Wall, the Czech firm Škoda was taken over by Volkswagen. In 1980, Vickers plc acquired Rolls-Royce Motors, and both would subsequently be taken over themselves eighteen years later, one by BMW, the other by Volkswagen.

In July 1994, seven years after its first involvement, the Ford Motor Company consolidated its position in Aston Martin Lagonda by acquiring 100 percent ownership. Straight away, Ford decided to assemble all its more prestigious labels under the banner of the First Automotive Group, formed in 1999: this included two American brands of the old school, Lincoln and Mercury, alongside more recently acquired European firms: Volvo, Jaguar, Land Rover … and Aston Martin.

Aston Martin naturally wanted to defend its values of excellence and exclusivity within this association, but it also had to become more mainstream, as it was now part of a powerful industrial group. The idea of creating a more affordable model, which had been kicking around for several years, resurfaced. With Ford at the helm, this plan became feasible by creating a creating a synergy between Jaguar and Aston Martin. Firstly, at the level of production, which was reorganised accordingly. The future Aston Martin would be manufactured at Bloxham, near Banbury in Oxfordshire, in a factory formerly used by JaguarSport to assemble the very exclusive XJ 220. There was spare capacity because production of the supercar had been halted due to a lack of customers.

In order to achieve higher production targets, Aston Martin would have to create a more accessible product. This providential model had already acquired the label NPX.

## TWR Partners with Aston Martin

The inclusion of Aston Martin Lagonda in the Ford stable, followed by the acquisition of Jaguar Cars in November 1989, would result in the rationalisation of production and product definition. At the time, Jaguar was working on a replacement for the XJ-S, which had never managed to shake off comparisons to the legendary E-Type. The programme, covering the XJ 41 (coupé) and XJ 42 (convertible), was launched in the early 1980s in an attempt to revive the spirit of the E-Type. Equipped with a six-cylinder engine, these seductive cars, designed by Keith Helfet at Jaguar, took their inspiration from a concept car unveiled by Pininfarina in 1978. Their development took several years, and a number of prototypes were built by Karmann in Germany.

The style of the Jaguar XJ 42 would influence that of the DB7.

Ford's takeover of Jaguar put a definitive stop to the XJ 41/42 project. The American management was reassessing everything with an aim of achieving standardisation across the group. It launched the new X 100 programme, which would culminate in the XK 8 in 1996, and gave a foretaste of future link-ups with Aston Martin's NPX project, which was also already underway.

It seemed logical that the two grand touring cars, the Aston Martin DB7 and the Jaguar XK 8, should share the same platform while carefully distinguishing themselves by their style and motorisation. The development of the DB7 was entrusted to TWR, which was set up in 1976 in Kidlington by Tom Walkinshaw, a sturdy chap with the lived-in features and stocky figure of Spencer Tracy.

Born on a Scottish farm in 1946, he had preserved much of the gruff, no-nonsense character of his rural childhood. His early career as a driver brought him some success, but it was his skills as an engineer that led him to open a workshop under the name of Tom Walkinshaw Racing (TWR). He fitted out racing cars for Mazda, Rover and Jaguar. After a succession of victories, links between Jaguar and TWR grew stronger. Together, they developed prototypes which dominated the Le Mans 24 Hours in 1988 and 1990, then TWR took care of the production of the XJ 220 and XJR 15 supercars.

TWR and Aston Martin formed an association in turn through the entity Aston Martin Oxford, which was charged with developing the DB7.

## IAN CALLUM: THE DB7 MAN

A graduate of the Royal College of Art, Ian Callum plied his trade at Jaguar after having worked for Aston Martin.

The style of the DB7, which was one of its most attractive features, owed a lot to Ian Callum. Born in 1954, a graduate of the Royal College of Art in London, Ian Callum began his career at Ford in 1979. He was sent to Turin to the bodywork builder Ghia which, like Jaguar and Aston Martin, belonged to the American company. After two years in Italy, 1988–1990, Ian Callum was then appointed by Jaguar to take the place of Geoff Lawson, who had been struck down by illness in June 1999.

The DB7 in its original version, equipped with a six-cylinder engine.

# THE DB7 TAKES ON
# A NEW SEGMENT (1993–1999)

Undeniably the DB7 had many things in common with Jaguar's contemporary models. However, it is received wisdom at Aston Martin that most of the genes were inherited from them.

Leaving such disputes to one side, it has to be acknowledged that the design of the DB7 is masterful. Few cars have enjoyed such longevity without acquiring wrinkles and appearing dated and stylistically outmoded. The DB7 was different from its contemporaries. Moreover, it is hard to imagine it painted in red or yellow. Its subtle lines are accentuated by refined and discreet tones, preferably the metallic almond green of the Aston racers.

The first version was driven by a six-cylinder engine which generated 335 hp, and a dual overhead camshaft unit that derived from Jaguar's AJ 6 type, but was here supercharged by an Eaton compressor. The semi-monocoque steel structure was also derived from a Jaguar platform. The mechanical base was resolutely modern with its four-wheel drive.

In July 1996, the DB7 came into being: it was fitted with airbags and had exchanged some body parts that were moulded in composite materials for steel. But already, a major evolution was taking place. The DB7 retired in May 1999 to make way for the DB7 Vantage.

## The DB7 Volante (1996–1999)

When the DB7 Volante was unveiled simultaneously at the Detroit and Los Angeles Auto Shows, in January 1996, Aston Martin made no secret of the primary destination of this convertible model: the sunny climes of Florida and California. Not surprisingly, this heavier, less aerodynamic version handled more moderately than the coupé. But it combined all the traditional elements associated with the British lifestyle: Connolly leather, walnut woodwork (or on request oak, elm or maple) and Wilson wool carpeting.

## The DB7 Vantage (1999)

A Vantage version of the DB7 was offered from March 1999, but this time there was more at stake in the name than a simple boost to the basic engine. Now it indicated a radically new mechanics … and much more. It involved a 'V' type twelve-cylinder 6-litre engine that delivered 420 hp. On the cusp of the third millennium, there were only six constructors who sold models equipped with the V12: BMW, Ferrari, Lamborghini, Mercedes-Benz, Rolls-Royce and Toyota.

A DB7 convertible tailor-made for the American market.

**Top:** The DB7 Vantage Volante came out at the same time as the coupé. **Middle left:** On board the DB7 Vantage, wood veneer was replaced with carbon fibre. **Middle right:** Unveiling of the Aston Martin V12 in April 1994. **Above:** A small inscription allows the DB7 to be identified from behind.

The Vanquish was the last model to be produced in the workshops at Newport Pagnell, where Aston Martin had first set up in the 1950s.

The new engine had been conceived by the Ford Research and Vehicle Technology Group with the assistance of Cosworth Technology. At Ford there had been talk of twelve cylinders for several years; what had been a dream was now real.

Many spectacular concept cars had boasted of using this type of mechanics. The Aston Martin Lagonda Vignale set the ball rolling in 1993, the official documentation announcing "a revolutionary idea for a V12 engine". In fact, this was made up of two 60° V6 blocs of modest extraction, the 'Duratec' equipping the Ford Mondeo.

The V12 obtained this way had a capacity of 6 litres and could deliver 400 hp at 6,000 rpm. A number of American concept cars proudly claimed to have similar propulsion units: the spider Ford Indigo (January 1996) and the Berlinetta GT 90, but these used a V12 open at 90° not 60°, and so were elaborated from V8 engines.

The main distinctive features of the DB7 Vantage presented at the Geneva Car Show in 1999 are the large round projectors added under the headlights. Unusually, the Volante convertible was launched at the same time as the coupé.

# THE TOP-OF-THE-RANGE VANQUISH

Aston Martin exhibited the Vantage project at the Detroit Auto Show in January 1998. Its contours, drawn by Ian Callum, are very different from those of the DB7: less slender, more aggressive, it announced a new top-of-the-range model which would carry the flame of the Virages.

A little over three years later, in March 2001, the project took solid form when the Vanquish was presented at the Geneva Car Show. It set out to be more exclusive than the DB7: that was its main raison d'être. It had its own chassis, but its engine, extrapolated from that of the DB7 Vantage, offered superior power: 460 hp. It was served by a six-speed sequential gearbox operated by paddle levers. When sitting at the wheel, you can't help but feel that you are in an exceptional car, made by hand. Some of the Vanquishes (ninety-four) were supplied with the Sport Dynamic Pack, which made them more incisive when it came to suspension and steering.

In October 2004, the Vanquish evolved into the Vanquish S, endowed with a 520 hp engine, which would finally bow out in July 2007. It would turn out to be the last model produced at the old factory in Newport Pagnell. It was in these historic workshops that the 1,503 units of the Vanquish and the 1,086 units of the Vanquish S were assembled.

**Above:** More brutal and more exclusive than the DB7 Vantage, the Vanquish was aimed at a different clientele. **Following pages:** The Vanquish S was at the top-of-the-range in 2004.

Compared to the DB7 Vantage, the DB7 GT offered a more sporting and rigorous dynamic behaviour.

## The DB7 GT and GTA (2002–2003)

At the Birmingham Motor Show in October 2002, Aston Martin unveiled the DB7 GT and GTA, the last episodes in the DB7 adventure. The progress made was obvious to anyone who drove it. Thanks to the extra 15 hp (435 as opposed to 420 hp), the cars had moved on from grand touring coupés to real full-bodied sports cars. The replacement of the shock absorbers was a decisive factor. Firmer and more progressive, they developed damping laws that made it possible to refine the dynamic behaviour. The roll that was still a persistent feature of the Vantage had virtually disappeared in the GT. The steering was more precise thanks to the choice of Bridgestone low-face tyres. The DB7 GT benefitted from Brembo discs, 335 mm diameter at the front and 330 mm at the back, which ensured fantastic braking. A small-diameter AP dual-disc clutch replaced the single-disc. Externally, the DB7 GT was recognisable by its radiator grille, its bonnet openings, its wheels and its rear spoiler. Internally, especially striking were the openwork pedals and the distinctive dark oak woodwork.

At the same time as the DB7 GT, Aston Martin launched the DB7 GTA. It was exactly the same car in terms of running gear. Unlike the GT, it was fitted with a five-speed automatic transmission coupled to the engine (420 hp) of the DB7 Vantage. In total, 6,910 DB7s were made, divided up as follows:

- DB7 with six-cylinder engine: 1,578 produced (529 with BV5);

- DB7 Vantage with V12 engine: 2,091 produced;

- DB7 Volante (convertible): 879 produced;

- DB7 Vantage Volante: 2,059 produced;

- DB7 GT: 191 produced;

- DB7 GTA: 112 produced.

# BERTONE'S JET 2 (2004)

Unveiled at the Geneva Car Show in 2004, this special bodywork was named the Jet 2 in honour of the first Jet created by Bertone in 1961. It rested on a Vanquish platform, elongated by 21 cm to a length of 467.5 cm. "By preserving all the mechanical elements, we have been able to create a radically different car simply by changing its garb, that is, its bodywork," explained Roberto Piatti, the managing director of Stile Bertone. The Jet 2 borrowed the windshield, deck and doors from the Vanquish, allowing it to keep the original certification. Aston Martin gave Stile Bertone free rein. "The Jet 2 had to look like an Aston Martin, that was our principal concern," said Giuliano Biasio, the head of external design. "So the dilemma was to marry the strong identity of Aston Martin, marked by its supple forms, with the style of Bertone, characterised by tight lines and a geometrical structure." The rear was characteristic of the Bertone style, with its sharp angles and the glazing that seamlessly combined the rear window and the tail lights in a single unit. The design of the rear integrated harmoniously with the overall balance and inspired Ferrari. For a few weeks, the Jet 2 was loaned to Maranello, and a few months later, the Ferrari FF appeared, with a profile modelled on that of the Jet 2. The lengthening of the wheelbase made it possible to provide emergency seating at the back. The windscreen was visually extended by a glazed pavilion with a central band inserted in it. The interior was defined by David Wilkie, who had been head of this sector at Stile Bertone since May 2003, having worked for nearly fifteen years at Ghia. "We imagined that the owner of a car like this would also be a lover of beautiful boats, and we also tried to recreate the feel of runabouts from the 1970s." Hence the intensive use of polished wood, as pleasant to touch as it is to look at. Even the floor was clad in wood, pear wood to be precise. The seats and the central console originated in the DB9.

The profile of the Jet 2 by Bertone would inspire the design of the Ferrari FF.

The DBS came to an end with the Ultimate series.

# DB9: A PERIOD OF RATIONALISATION

Aston Martin Lagonda remained under the wing of the Ford Motor Company for twenty years. Before they parted company in 2007, they had created a new generation of cars which would be rolled out in multiple formats.

For Aston Martin, the DB9 marked the entry into a new era. It was part of a restructured range based on the flexibility of a mechanical light alloy platform called the 'VH' (Vertical & Horizontal). This modular base could be used to create very different models simply by varying the wheelbase and the tracks. The DB9 therefore shared its structure with the more compact V8 Vantage, the Rapide saloon and the very exclusive DBS.

# THE DB9 INAUGURATES
# THE VH GENERATION (2003–2008)

Developed under new president Ulrich Bez, who arrived at Aston Martin in 2000, the DB9 was the successor to the DB7. It was structured around a 'transaxle' architecture, that is, with the gearbox and the differential placed on the rear axle and connected to the engine through a carbon shaft rotating in an aluminium tube. The suspension remained classic, with double-forged aluminium wishbones and conventional, free-running shock absorbers. The compromise between comfort and road holding was perfect; the filtration guaranteed the passengers' well-being without causing the damping to compromise on the rigour needed to guide the heavy machine. The dynamic behaviour was precise, consistent and always predictable. A battery of driving aids performed its function discreetly; emergency brake assist and traction control were properly used.

The DB9 profited from a successful synergy within the Premier Automotive Group. Volvo dealt with matters concerning passive safety and the electrical equipment, while both Aston Martin and Jaguar were experts in the use of aluminium.

The performance of the V12 engine was improved to deliver 450 hp, where the DB7 had had to settle for 420 hp and the DB7 with 435 hp. It was assembled at Cosworth Technology, a subsidiary of the Volkswagen group, but things soon reverted to normal when the production of the mechanics was transferred to Ford in Cologne.

A timeless line that lost none of its beauty over the course of the thirteen years the DB9 was produced.

**Top:** The DB9 is harmonious from every angle. **Above:** An original sketch by Henrik Fisker for the DB9.

Progressive and linear, the V12 was fundamentally non-violent. Aston Martin set great store by its six-speed ZF automatic transmission, which could be selected manually thanks to paddle levers behind the steering wheel. The transmission and the differential were furnished by the Graziano Trasmissioni Group, a supplier of Ferrari and Maserati. The choice of automation showed that driving comfort was a top priority.

In terms of ergonomics, the DB9 was a major step forward with its spacious, well-lit and airy interior. The choice of wood was original. As well as the usual walnut and the less conventional mahogany, the much rarer bamboo was used. With its matte finish, it offered lightness and transparency and created subtle harmonies with certain skin tones. The leather was provided by the Scottish firm Bridge of Weir Leather Company, who had replaced Connolly. The odd touch of aluminium added a more technological feel to the tonal range.

# HENRIK FISKER: HEAD OF DESIGN
# FROM 2001 TO 2005

Henrik Fisker played an influential role in asserting the Aston Martin style.

Henrik Fisker arrived at Aston Martin in August 2001 and was immediately tasked with giving a face to the models of the generation established on the 'VH' platform. The first on the list was the prototype AM V8 Vantage, followed swiftly by the DB9. For Henrik Fisker, the difficulty was to give a distinct identity to each model. A subtle task, which he acquitted with aplomb. He made the following distinction between the two projects: "With the AM V8 Vantage, which had to compete with the Porsche 911, we wanted to create a compact, squat, powerful design, to give it an aggressive character. With the DB9, the objective was to develop more fluid lines and a more generous space, because we wanted to offer a large GT evoking elegance and comfort."

"Everything depends on the accuracy of the proportions," said Henrik Fisker, "to differentiate itself from the AM V8 Vantage, the DB9 is based on a long wheelbase. The front and rear overhangs remain large and equitable in order to give the DB9 very balanced proportions." The surfaces are extremely smooth, unlike the sides of the AM V8 Vantage, which are split by a groove, and unlike the profile of the Vanquish, which has very prominent haunches and more contained cantilevers.

Born 10 August 1963, Henrik Fisker studied at the Art Center College of Design in Pasadena. Between 1989 and 1992, he worked for the studio BMW Technik in Munich. He then crossed the Atlantic to take charge of Designworks in Newbury Park, the Californian subsidiary set up by BMW. It was on his watch that the Z07 project was conceived, which would later result in the Z8. In September 2001, Henrik Fisker was appointed director of the London-based studio Ingeni, which Ford wanted to use as an experimental laboratory, but this fizzled out. After the closure of Ingeni, in 2003, Fisker was appointed director of the design studio Ford had set up in California, his last post before Aston Martin. He would stay there until 2005, after which he set up his own company and launched the extraordinary Karma.

In September 2003, the DB9 moved to new premises in Gaydon, a village in Warwickshire, about 20 km south of Coventry. This ultramodern factory, surrounded by moats, was designed by Weedom Architects: it was built on the site of a former RAF base and incorporated production units for Jaguar and Land-Rover, as well as housing the British Motor Heritage Centre, a museum that paid homage to the work of all the British firms.

The old workshops in Newport Pagnell, with their dark brick walls, would henceforth be used purely to restore historic models.

## The DB9 Volante (2004)

One finds oneself constantly showering praise on the style of Aston Martins. This would very much remain the case when the pure lines of the DB9 Volante were first revealed. The visitors to the Detroit Auto Show in January 2004 were the first to catch a glimpse the new machine. It would, however, be a few months before anyone was able to drive a DB9 Volante, as the engineers had to reinforce the rigidity of the VH structure, which was prone to the specific issues created by an open car.

 In addition, the Volante had the same technical characteristics as the coupé, apart from the suspension, which was more supple given its role as a tourer. The usual disadvantage of convertibles is their weight, but that was less of an issue in the Volante, which was just 100 kg heavier than the DB9 coupé, weighing in at 1,815 kg.

The DB9 was even purer in its Volante version, but probably less stereotypical.

# The DB9 in Constant Evolution (2004–2016)

At the Geneva Car Show in 2004, the DB9 showed off its first significant evolution. Retouches to the exterior were fairly minimal and were limited to enlarged mirrors, a grille that now had only five horizontal bars instead of seven, and 19-inch wheels. The 5.9-litre V12 engine carved out a few extra horsepower to reach 470 hp. The suspension was improved by the adaptive damper system (ADS) and the use of Bilstein shock absorbers.

In June 2010, the DB9 was given a new front shield on which the design of the air intakes had been modified. For the 2011 and 2012 vintages, the DB9 would have to amicably coexist with the Virage, which, while adopting a similar silhouette, was more sophisticated and more efficient. But the Virage had a short life, its success mitigated no doubt by this very same, and rather flagrant, resemblance.

For the 2013 vintage, with the Virage no longer on the scene, the DB9 found itself once more alone at the heart of the range, in between the V8 Vantage and the DBS. With the exception of a discreet spoiler integrated into the boot, the DB9 was aligned aesthetically with the Virage, with its stretched headlights, filled with LEDs, and an enlarged air intake under the shield. The engine environment as well as the fenders and bonnet had been reworked to meet pedestrian impact standards. These modifications increased the rigidity of the structure by 20 percent. The wheel rims, with Pirelli P Zero tyres, were increased from 19 to 20 inches, the Brembo brakes had large carbon/ceramic discs as standard and the controlled suspension offered three damping laws (Comfort, Sport and Track). The V12, with variable intake and exhaust timing, now boasted 517 hp and 620 Nm of torque.

The most successful of all the DB9s was probably the DB9 GT, which put in an appearance at Goodwood in June 2015. As well as its engine ramped up to 540 hp, the DB9 GT had the sophisticated infotainment system of the Vanquish. The story of the DB9 reached its end in July 2016.

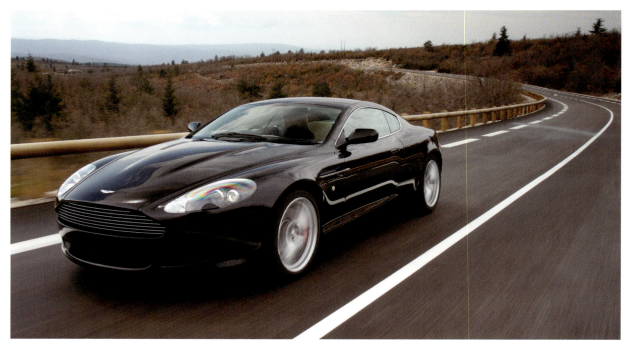

A DB9 equipped with the Sports Pack in July 2006.

At the end of 2012, for the 2013 vintage, the DB9 underwent significant visible changes in the optics and shield.

# ULRICH BEZ

Ulrich Bez was a rather unique boss; the people around him would know what mood he was in at any given moment by the way he changed his glasses! More seriously, he was one of those industry leaders who loves cars and knows them inside out. A graduate in aeronautical engineering from the University of Stuttgart, Bez began his career in 1982 with BMW Technik GmbH. He was thirty-nine years old at the time and was instrumental in the establishment of a unit tasked with developing fringe projects and initiating futuristic or ground-breaking products, like the Z1. He then spent four years at Porsche (1988–1992), where he was involved in developing roadsters and racing cars. Following this, he headed up engineering and development at Daewoo Motors from 1993 to 1998, before taking up the reins at Aston Martin Lagonda in July 2000. He would remain as CEO until June 2013. He stayed on as chair of the board for a further two years. There was life after Aston Martin: Bez was involved in a number of businesses: Alset Global, Magnis Resources ASX, Umbez-Consulting and, since January 2020, Keyou GmbH.

**Top left:** The special series DB9 LM, 124 of which were constructed after September 2007 to mark the victory of the DBR9 in the GT1 class at the Le Mans 24 Hours. **Top right:** In June 2010, the shield was modified on the DB9. **Middle left:** The DB9 Volante with modified shield and headlights in October 2012. **Middle right:** The interior style kept its central motif, so characteristic on this 2012 model. **Above:** The Virage offered both coupé and convertible models.

# THE VIRAGE (2011)

Unveiled at the Geneva Car Show in 2011 in a rather surprising orange livery, the Virage—a new car with a familiar name—took its place in the range between the DB9 and the DBS. At first sight it was difficult to distinguish the design of the Virage from that of the DB9, even though all the bodywork panelling was new. The most obvious difference concerned the decluttered front shield highlighted by a blade of carbon fibre. The grille had a somewhat accentuated design. The projectors were trimmed with a ramp of LEDs and the rear shield incorporated a diffuser. Lighter than the DB9 (1,785 kg), the Virage had carbon fibre wings, but the openings were still in aluminium. It inherited the 20-inch wheels with Pirelli P Zero tyres, the carbon/ceramic brakes and the controlled damping of the DBS. This V12 drew 497 hp and was coupled with six-speed automatic gearbox called the Touchtronic II. There were two interior configurations available: 2+2 with cramped rear seats or a simple two-seater, with the folding seats replaced by a luggage area. The Virage dropped out of the catalogue after only eighteen months, and only 1,044 units (656 coupés and 388 convertibles) were produced.

**Above:** Although it was positioned between the DB9 and the DBS, the Virage was visually too close to the DB8. **Following pages:** The DB9 GT with its style and speed brought to an end the saga of the DB9.

The final avatar of the DB9, the Rapide saloon launched in 2009.

## The Rapide or the DB9 Transformed into a Saloon (2009)

The first appearance of the Aston Martin Rapide was at the Detroit Auto Show in January 2006, and it went on the market in September 2009. It was based on the DB9 coupé, from which it derived its charm and character, with a flatter silhouette. Of course, it also had the ergonomics of a coupé in terms of accessibility, driving position and space in the rear seats. In the early years, serial production was entrusted to the firm of Magna Steyr in Graz, Austria, but later brought home to Gaydon in autumn 2012. In total 2,872 Rapides were built.

In February 2013, the Rapide was replaced by the Rapide S. It was immediately recognisable by its front face with its full-height grille; what wasn't immediately visible was that it sat on the VH platform in its Gen4 execution with its adaptive suspension and the latest safety standards, especially for protecting pedestrians in the event of an impact.

At the rear, the spoiler that punctuated the boot was more prominent. The option of a 'carbon pack' allowed a few touches of the precious composite on the deflector, diffuser, rear optics and mirror shell. On the inside, also as an option, the Rapide offered a brand-new type of perforated leather, treated in two colours, red and black. The standard woodwork was in walnut, but bamboo, oak, mahogany or a piano lacquer finish were all available.

# THE JET 2+2 BY BERTONE (2013)

The Jet 2+2 photographed at the Sacra di San Michele, perched on top of Monte Pirchiriano, the Benedictine abbey that formed the backdrop to the film *The Name of the Rose*, directed by Jean-Jacques Annaud in 1986.

At the Geneva Car Show in 2013, Bertone unveiled a unique car made at the request of Barry Weir, a British property magnate. A Rapide turned into an estate car, it used the original cell, with its sides and doors, but had a redesigned rear. The roof line had been elongated and raised, providing ample space for the rear seats.

The Jet 2+2 was constructed on the base of a 2012 Rapide and retained its 476 hp engine, although its face was that of the Rapide S. The two rear seats could fold up to clear a large loading space surfaced in walnut. The Jet 2+2 had been built in the new 'Bertone Officina' department in Capri, which was dedicated to one-off productions.

The Rapide S had a new twelve-cylinder AM11 type engine with 17 percent more power (558 hp as opposed to 477 hp). Despite these improvements, the car was greener, since the $CO_2$ emissions had been reduced to 23 b/km. In August 2014, the Rapide S was fitted with the eight-speed ZF Touchtronic gearbox.

The series of saloons came to an end with the Rapide AMR, which was limited to a production run of 210 units. It employed the V12 engine from the Vantage GT12, which provided 603 hp and 630 Nm.

The Rapide S also served as the base for prototypes experimenting with new sources of energy. The Hybrid Hydrogen competed in the Nürburgring 24 Hours in the E1-XP category, which was exclusive to experimental technologies. Four carbon tanks (two in the boot and two in the passenger compartment) could store 3.5 kg of hydrogen in a gaseous state at a pressure of 350 bar. It was able to complete a complete lap of the circuit feeding off hydrogen, that is, without any noise or rejection; for the rest of the race, the car drew on its petrol supply. The technical aspects were developed in cooperation with the Austrian firm Alset Global.

At the Auto China Show in Shanghai in April 2019, Aston Martin presented the definitive version of the Rapide E, pinning down its technical characteristics (950 hp delivered by two electric engines), and announced a production run limited to 155 units. This was never completed.

**Top:** The more efficient and more aggressive Rapide S tried to revive sales of the saloon but without success. **Above:** The Rapide E, or the promise of a large electric-powered road car.

# A CHANGE OF OWNERSHIP

Well before the of sub-prime mortgage crisis that would throw the world of finance and economics into turmoil in 2008, the Ford Motor Company took measures that allowed it to survive the chaos better than the other two of the American big three: GM and Chrysler.

Appointed chair in September 2006, Alan Mullaly decided to restructure the business and dismantle the Premium Automotive Group by dropping most of the brands acquired by his predecessor: Aston Martin was sold in 2007, Jaguar taken on by the Tata group (2008), Mercury shut down (2010), Volvo sold to Geely (2010), and Mazda would become independent (2014).

Ulrich Bez negotiated the exit of Aston Martin Lagonda and its takeover by an investment group made up of David Richards, John Sinders and the Kuwait-based banks Investment Dar and Adeen Investment.

## THE LAGONDA TARAF (2015)

At Geneva in March 2015 Aston Martin discreetly unveiled (on the stand but in a private room!) a special edition of the Rapide 5 which had previously been shown to a select few in Dubai in December 2014. The Taraf bore the Lagonda logo, and its lines diverged from those of the DB9 to create a more conventional profile. Initially envisaged only for the Middle East market, it was also distributed in Europe, with approximately 120 cars produced.

The Taraf was a limited series of the Lagonda with a more conventional look.

# DAVID RICHARDS

When on 12 March 2007 Aston Martin published the list of members of the consortium who had just bought the business, the name of David Richards was near the head of it. He was a major figure in the modern world of auto sport. After partnering Ari Vatanen and sharing the rally world championship with him in 1981, Richards himself drove a car made by his own company in 1984. Prodrive, as his firm was known, soon hitched its name and its destiny to a number of brands: Subaru (with six rally world championships), BMW, Alfa Romeo and Ford in the British Touring Car championship, BAR-Honda in Formula 1 in 2004, then Ferrari. The old 550 GTS prepared by Prodrive in 2005 was more efficient than the more recent 575 GTC developed at Maranello! Typical one-upmanship on the part of the cynical David Richards! Then Prodrive took over the Grand Touring programme at Aston Martin, and so got one foot on the inside.

David Richards alongside Ulrich Bez.

## The Return of the DBS (2007–2012)

A star of the future played its first role in an action film: the DBS made its debut in *Casino Royale*, which was released in November 2006. After this first appearance in the world of James Bond, the DBS was shown at Pebble Beach in August 2007, a few weeks after its commercial launch at the Frankfurt Car Show in 2007.

The new DBS wasn't a natural successor to the DBS of 1967; it succeeded the Vanquish at the top of the range, and so was among the most exclusive and expensive models.

In turn, it adopted the VH modular platform and draped itself in a more voluptuous style than that of the Vanquish. Its lines were brought up to date and subtly softened. The profile followed a smooth and continuous line that no longer featured the abrupt angle of the rear wing as was the case on its predecessor. The new DBS inaugurated a number of innovations at Aston Martin: the installation of ventilated carbon/ceramic brakes and the replacement of aluminium with carbon fibre for several body parts (bonnet, boot lid, doors and front fenders), saving 30 kg.

# THE V8 VANTAGE

This book has as its common thread the models bearing the initials of David Brown, so the smaller Aston Martins fall outside of its scope. However, we cannot overlook this V8 Vantage, which played a crucial role in the success of the brand.

The AM305 project was launched by Ulrich Bez with the aim of competing with bestsellers such as the Porsche 911. The AM V8 Vantage appeared at the 2003 Auto Show in Detroit as a concept car designed under the direction of Henrik Fisker.

The definitive version was unveiled two years later in March 2005 in Geneva.

A roadster was added to the range in December 2006, then the coupé started its sporting career by competing in the Nürburgring 24 Hours in 2006. Since then, the Vantage has been very active on all the racetracks of the world: both the V8 Vantage GTE entered by the factory in the World Endurance Championship (WEC) and the V12 Vantage GT3 offered to private ecuries for the FIA GT1 world championship and the Blancpain Endurance Series. In the roadster range, the Vantage became available from March 2009 with the twelve-cylinder engine of the DB9.

A new generation of compact cars began with the V8 Vantage.

Top left: The interior ambience of the DBS aimed to be more opulent than that of the DB9. Top right: The style of the DBS is softer than that of the Vanquish which it replaced. Above: The DBS in its Volante convertible form.

Over the course of the DBS's career, Aston Martin added more special series to feed the appetite of its well-off clientele: Carbon Black, Carbon Edition and Ultimate, and ended up producing a total of 2,533 coupés.

Unlike the Vanquish, the new DBS came in a convertible, which was presented at the Geneva Car Show in 2009. It complied with the technical definition of the coupé from which it took the 510 hp engine, allowing it to position itself a cut above the DB9 Volante. Manufacture of the Vanquish Volante ended during summer 2012 with 846 having been produced.

# THE AMR-ONE PROTOTYPE (2011)

The return of Aston Martin to international competition with a machine of its own conception should have been one of the highlights of the ILMC (International Le Mans Cup). It came as something of a disillusionment, then, that the AMR-One was one of the great disappointments of the year.

On 1 March 2011, at midnight, Aston Martin unveiled with great fanfare its new prototype, designed under the leadership of George Howard-Chappell, who worked for Prodrive before becoming Aston Martin Racing's Team Principal.

Some of their technical decisions were surprising when set against those of their principal rivals. The open bodywork had high sides and a linear design to create an optimal drag coefficient (Cx). The engine was a direct injection inline six-cylinder, turbocharged, 540 hp. The six-speed gearbox, supplied by Xtrac, was arranged crosswise. It had assisted electrical steering, a light and compact solution, but less precise than the hydraulic system.

Their racing debut ended with an eleventh place at Le Castellet, but poor performances in the preliminary tests at Le Mans led the team to give up at Spa. At the Le Mans 24 Hours the two cars they entered were the first to quit at the end of the second and fourth laps. An experience to forget.

Complete fiasco for the Aston Martin AMR-One in the colours of Gulf at the Le Mans 24 Hours in 2011.

The style of the DBS Superleggera was more aggressive than that of the Vanquish that preceded it.

# DB11: A GENTLE REVOLUTION

After the recession of 2008, the luxury brands had to take a hard look at themselves. Aston Martin Lagonda was no exception. The company surmounted its difficulties by a series of bold initiatives.

The failure of the Lehman Brothers bank on 15 September 2008 led to the collapse of the financial markets. Immediately, the crisis spread to the wider economy and became global. Not easy, in this context, for an independent manufacturer to survive outside the industrial mainstream. This was the reality faced by Aston Martin Lagonda after being released by Ford in March 2007. After that, a group of shareholders took over the company, but the balance of power would continue to evolve.

# THE RETURN OF THE VANQUISH

Rather unimaginatively, Aston Martin Lagonda reintroduced the Vanquish name for the successor to the DBS, which itself had replaced the first Vanquish. The new generation indicated the direction of the style that Marek Reichman would impart to the entire range. First glimpsed in May 2012 during the Villa d'Este Concours d'Élégance, the Vanquish was officially unveiled on 20 June.

Its style respected the spirit of the firm, but with a wider mouth, a stretched gaze, more sculpted flanks. The side motif was accentuated by a thick arrow that faded at the end. The body belt followed the undulation of the wings and all around the car, the more technical parts—front bumper, sill and rear skirt—had dark reflections of carbon. The stern was longer and rounder. It had better ergonomics and more capacity in the luggage compartment. The customer could choose between two setups: simply two seats, or with two emergency seats at the back.

The Vanquish inaugurated the fourth generation (Gen4) of the VH platform. Phase I was the Vantage, phase II the DBS, phase III the Rapide, the Virage and the One-77. Gen4 was characterised by its intensive use of carbon, which improved torsional rigidity. The V12 was housed lower in the chassis and now provided 565 hp. Three damping modes were available with the Adaptive Damping System (ADS): normal, sport and track. At the Los Angeles Auto Show in November 2016, the Vanquish gave way to the Vanquish S, endowed with 595 hp. The Vanquish Volante arrived in June 2013; 1,001 would be produced before it in turn was replaced by the Vanquish S Volante in March 2017.

The 2012 Vanquish had a familiar name, but its silhouette was original.

**Top:** A spectacular sketch for the Vanquish signed by Miles Nurnberger. **Above:** The Vanquish Volante complemented the coupé from 2013.

# A NEW ADMINISTRATIVE FRAMEWORK

In December 2012, the cards were reshuffled: the investment fund Investindustrial came on the scene and became the main shareholder of Aston Martin Lagonda by taking the 37.5 percent stake that was previously held by The Investment Dar (TID). This Italian company, directed by Andrea Bonomi, had sold Ducati to Audi.

A year later, on 19 December 2013, Aston Martin Lagonda signed a fateful agreement. They formed an alliance with the Daimler group, which took up a stake of 5 percent in Aston Martni Lagonda with a view to a technical partnership. The cooperation covered electronic safety and information systems and the supply of an engine designed at AMG.

There were changes in personnel too. In October 2014, Andy Palmer took charge of Aston Martin Lagonda, filling the post that had been left vacant since the departure of Ulrich Bez in November 2013. Andy Palmer had been shaped by twenty-three years of rationalisation at Nissan, where he was vice president in charge of planning before his departure.

# MAREK REICHMAN

Marek Reichman became executive vice president in November 2017.

The award ceremony for the Gentlemen Driver category at the Concours d'Élégance was taking place in the soft evening air of a royal garden in Marrakesh. All of the members of the jury were dressed up to the nines: dress code black tie. Everyone except Marek Reichman. He had no time for convention. He arrived draped in a *djellaba* that he had bought earlier in the souk. Marek Reichman is not a conformist, he is British. His job since June 2005 had been to shake up Aston Martin. He had slipped through the net of the restructuring programme. He had been there in the time of Ford and Ulrich Bez and survived them both. He even became executive vice president in November 2017.

Born in 1966 in Sheffield, UK, Marek Reichman prepared himself for the fray by attending Teesside University in Middlesborough and the Royal College of Art in London. In 1991, he started his career at Rover, which was taken over by BMW three years later. This was a springboard to working at BMW's Designworks studio in California in 1995. "In February 1996, five months after I joined BMW, they put me in charge of the third generation of the Range Rover. It's one of the pieces of work I'm most proud of." In September 1999, Reichman went to work for Ford in Detroit, then the owners of Aston Martin. After managing the design of the Lincoln-Mercury and joining the design department of Ford North America, where he was responsible for interior design and strategy, he was sent to England in May 2005 to head the Aston Martin creative studio, where he succeeded Henrik Fisker. The two men had worked together at Designworks.

Sax player, Radiohead fan, collector of beautiful watches and powerful motorcycles, experienced kayaker, Marek seemed more streetwise than his customers. He would bring them up to speed. In December 2007, a brand-new studio was set up at Gaydon.

First public appearance of the One-77 at the Villa d'Este Concours d'Élégance in 2009.

# THE ONE-77 (2009–2012)

This is the first project that can be attributed to Marek Reichman. Exhibited, albeit covered up (!), at the Mondial de l'Automobile in 2008, this magnificent machine was finally fully revealed at the Villa d'Este Concours d'Élégance in April 2009. Given its aspiration to exclusivity, the One-77's style was deliberately aggressive, because it had to display its marginality and its exclusive character. "Everything on the One-77 was exaggerated," Marek Reichman admits, "the style played on excess, on a disproportionately long bonnet, a flattened cabin, an aggressive face, and open gills all around the body."

The front shield incorporated two side air intakes like two shark gill slits, themselves extended by outsized slits continuing over the doors. The rear shield surmounted an imposing extractor. The central cell was made of carbon fibre by the Hungarian company Multimatic. On the technical side, the project manager, Chris Porritt, created a shell extended by aluminium cradles.

The V12, reworked by Cosworth Engineering, its weight reduced by 25 percent, had an increased capacity of 7.3 litres, which enabled it to produce 747 Nm and more than 750 hp. A new dry sump lubrication system lowered the centre of gravity. The monocoque chassis was, of course, made of carbon fibre. It was accompanied by some impressive so-called 'active' aerodynamic gear.

Only seventy-seven One-77s would be produced, and the last ones were delivered in summer 2012.

# THE VERY URBAN CYGNET (2009)

Aston Martin offered its clientele (and ultimately every Tom, Dick or Harry, contrary to expectation) a city car named Cygnet. Unveiled at the Geneva Car Show in 2010, the small contemporary Cygnet was no more no less than a personalised Toyota iQ: traditional radiator grille, front and rear bumpers, side decorative pattern, leather and Alcantara upholstery, piano lacquer finish on the dashboard. These adjustments were carried out in the workshops of Aston Martin. Options included a kit to lower the suspension and Bill Amberg travel accessories.

The Cygnet—here in the special 'Colette' series—provided an energy-efficient model in its range.

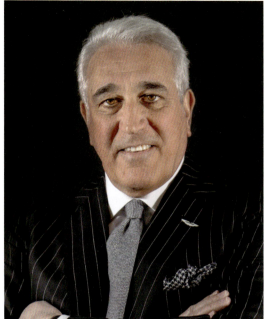

**Above left:** In 2018, the name of Aston Martin was applied once again to the nose of the Red Bull RB14. **Above right:** The Canadian millionaire Laurence Stroll became the big cheese at Aston Martin in 2020.

Realism required thinking about new sources of energy: in order to develop its electric engines, Aston Martin joined forces with the Chinese firm LeEco in 2016 to produce its electrified prototype based on the Rapide saloon.

Aston Martin Global Holdings Limited was incorporated on 30 July 2018 and converted into Aston Martin Global Holdings plc on 7 September 2018. There was an unexpected twist in January 2020, when a new investor showed an interest in the old brand. This was Lawrence Stroll, a Canadian businessman who had built his fortune on the distribution of ready-to-wear brands such as Ralph Lauren, Michael Kors and Tommy Hilfiger.

On 31 January 2020, the deal was made official: the group Yew Tree Overseas Ltd, led by Laurence Stroll, paid 316 million Canadian dollars (£182 million) to acquire 16.7 percent of Aston Martin Lagonda.

After a devaluation of the company, Yew Tree's contribution was revised downwards in April 2020 to £171 million for 25 percent of the capital, instead of £182 million for 16.7 percent. Omega Funds, a company of Swiss billionaire Ernesto Bertarelli, and ErsteAM, linked to Toto Wolff, boss of the Mercedes F1 team, also participated in the deal, and acquired 0.66 percent and 0.95 percent respectively of the voting rights. The Investindustrial fund was the second largest shareholder with 14.99 percent of the capital.

On 20 April 2020, Laurence Stroll took up the post of executive president of Aston Martin Lagonda Global Holdings plc. He immediately announced that Aston Martin would be taking part in Formula 1 from the start of the 2021 season. To do so, he turned to the Racing Point F1 team he had built in 2019 by taking over Force India. Previously, the Aston Martin name had been affixed to Red Bull Racing's single-seaters since 2016.

On 26 May 2020, the board announced the departure with immediate effect of the director general Andy Palmer. The vice president, Keith Stanton, stood in temporarily until 1 August, when Tobias Moers, the former director general of Mercedes-AMG, took up the role.

# THE CONCEPT CAR CC100 (2013)

This two-seater roadster, based on the Aston Martin V12 Vantage GT3, celebrated the centenary of the Aston Martin DBR1, which won the Le Mans and Nürburgring 24 Hour races in 1959. Its design bore the signature of Miles Nurnberger, the head of external design, answerable to Marek Reichman. Light, with a weight limit of 1,200 kg, thanks to a carbon fibre shell, the CC100 clocked up some impressive performances; 290 km/h and 0 to 100 in 4 seconds. This concept car was sold to a collector and a second car was ordered from the English firm.

The CC100 uncompromisingly takes up the theme of the roadster; the lack of windscreen was particularly noted by designers.

# THE VULCAN (2015)

In March 2015, Aston Martin offered a limited edition of twenty-four purely for use on private tracks … and not in any competitive race! A carbon shell, a six-speed sequential gearbox and carbon/ceramic brakes were among the features of this resolutely aggressive style. The engine, placed at the front, but very tucked in under the passenger compartment, was a 7-litre V12, which delivered 800 hp.

Resolutely aggressive, the Vulcan was a toy reserved for a very happy few who wanted to have fun on the circuits.

# The DB10 in *Spectre* (2015)

After driving the Vanquish in *Die Another Day* (2002) and the DBS in *Casino Royale* (2006) and *The Quantum of Solace* (2008), James Bond had a DB5 in *Skyfall* (2012). For *Spectre*, two specific prototypes were mentioned in the script: the Aston Martin DB10 for the secret agent and the Jaguar G-X75 for his rival.

The DB10, based on the V8 Vantage (4.7 litres, 426 hp), was specially created for the film and was never intended to be sold, even if its chunky, vigorous style prefigured that of the future Vantage of 2017. The DB10 was a merely virtual link between the DB9 and the DB11.

Ten were delivered to the production house. One of them was sold at auction by Christie's in London in February 2016 for £2,435,000.

Ten examples of the DB10 were made for the film *Spectre*.

Even in its preliminary sketches, the style of the DB11 exudes strength and voluptuousness.

# THE DB11: A TECHNOLOGICAL AND AESTHETIC BREAK WITH THE PAST (2016–)

The DB11 renewed with great panache that most precious quality of the Aston Martin: its indefinable elegance. Behind its harmonious contours, the DB11 conceals changes that have revolutionised the brand in the last few years. Notably in its design. Muscular wings, a feline bearing, sides lined with expressive wrinkles, a rounded backside. There is no shortage of easy, anthropomorphic metaphors to describe the aesthetics of the DB11.

Marek Reichman uses his own body to explain the change. He contorts himself to show the aerodynamic flows, he caresses the curves to show the musculature, leaps from one end to the other of the DB11 to illustrate how strength and voluptuousness go hand in hand, to emphasise the downstrokes and upstrokes that write the Aston Martin style of today.

Unveiled at a preview in March 2016, the DB11 respects the fundamental values of the brand: discretion and efficiency. All in halftones. A refined feel all over: no aggression here. Aston Martin offers a distinguished colour chart that oscillates between off-white and almost black navy, between 'soft tech' and the 'mysterious sport'. The 'intrepid sport' shade, the most daring, uses the orange colouring of cinnabar.

Just below the surface, the DB11 is truly revolutionary. It abandons the former atmospheric 6-litre V12 in favour of a 5.2-litre doubly turbocharged V12, providing 600 hp and managing its consumption thanks to the alternating activation of the two-cylinder banks.

**Top:** Against the backdrop of Honfleur, the style of the DB11 marks a radical break with the DB9. **Above:** The cockpit of the DB11 preserves the iconic console. **Following pages:** Less stripped back, more muscular: the style of the DB11.

In July 2017, Aston Martin provided a more affordable way to access the DB11: a 4-litre twin-turbo V8 engine which still offered 510 hp.

It was a logical development that the DB11 should appear in Volante form in October 2017. It was magnificent, of course, but 115 kg heavier, and was offered only with the V8 engine, which was lighter than the V12. Equally expected, an even more powerful version, embellished with the initials AMR for Aston Martin Racing, arrived in May 2018, coinciding with the inauguration of the new AMR Performance Centre department based at the Nürburgring. This progression signalled the arrival of the engineer Matt Becker from Lotus. The improvements were in the optimised chassis, the more rigorous suspension and an increased power of 630 hp.

## THE VANTAGE (2017–)

At the end of a successful career that began in 2003 in the form of a concept car, the 'small' Aston Martin in its V8 and V12 versions was replaced in November 2017 by a model with a more expressive style (reference AM6). Unfortunately, the 'lime essence' colour chosen for the launch was not the most flattering for a brand with a reputation for discretion! Under the bonnet, it had an engine from Mercedes-AMG, the result of an alliance with the Daimler group: a 4-litre V8 providing 510 hp. A sports version of the new Vantage appeared in 2018 under the acronym AMR. Its development was handled by Prodrive, under the direction of Dan Sayers, Aston Martin's technical director. The GTE was rolled out in 2018, the GT3 and the GT4 in 2019.

The new Vantage (AM6 generation) pitches up in the Sancerre region of France.

The DB11 Volante enters the pantheon of the world's most beautiful cars.

# A HOMAGE TO VICTOR GAUNTLETT

In memory of the man who led Aston Martin from 1981 to 1991, and later died in 2003, this prototype was produced by Department Q, which was responsible for special orders. It made its debut at the Hampton Court Palace Concours of Elegance in September 2020. This unique model adopted the lines of the V8 that was sold between 1977 and 1989, but gave them a great deal more heft. The Victor borrowed its structure and its V12 7.3-litre engine from the One-77, which achieved 848 hp after a stint at Cosworth. Its suspension and cockpit derived from the Vulcan, the internal décor fused tradition and modernity, with a combination of green and fawn leather, matte wood and carbon.

A postmodern style, evoking the 1980s, a homage to Victor Gauntlett.

The Volante version of the DBS Superleggera was one of the most powerful convertibles on the market.

# THE DBS SUPERLEGGERA (2018–)

The Vanquish passed the baton as the top-of-the-range front-engined Aston Martin to the DBS Superleggera in June 2018. It was first presented at the Roundhouse, in London. The lessons learned from the DB11 were here brought to an apogee, in the name of exclusivity. An aluminium platform and carbon body justified the Superleggera label, and its dry weight was limited to 1,693 kg, which guaranteed high-level performance: 282 km/h top speed and 0 to 100 in 3.4 seconds. In terms of style, Marek Reichman's team followed the tradition of the DB11 but gave it a more aggressive twist. The engine continued on its upward curve: with capacity increased to 5.2 litres, it now delivered 715 hp. The eight-speed ZF automatic transmission was still rear-mounted.

In April 2019, the convertible version of the DBS Superleggera was added; naturally, it was sublime. The hood deployed automatically in 16 seconds, but its dry weight was 1,863 kg as opposed to the coupé's 1,693 kg.

**Above left:** The gaping mouth of the DBS Superleggera. **Above right:** The interior décor of the DBS Superleggera combines luxury with technology.

# THE DBX EXPLORES
# NEW TERRITORY (2019–)

In 2015 the concept car DBX prefigured the arrival of an SUV in the range. It was an inevitable development for all the luxury car constructors. Whatever the inspiration was behind these four-wheel drives, even if they were considered incongruous, controversial or undesirable, it was clear that there was customer demand for the concept of 'off-road grand tourism'. After Porsche—a forerunner with its Cayenne—Bentley, Lamborghini, Maserati and Rolls-Royce had fallen in with the trend. Aston Martin joined them with the DBX, which rests on a brand-new platform made of bonded aluminium. It features a double wishbone front suspension combined with a multilink rear axle and electronic adaptive damping on each wheel. The DBX has an active four-wheel drive with variable torque distribution and height-adjustable air suspension. Presented at the Los Angeles Auto Show in November 2019, the DBX has been manufactured since July 2020 in the new St Athan factory in Wales created out of former RAF hangars near Cardiff.

**Top:** In March 2015, the concept car DBX reveals Aston Martin's interest in the world of SUVs. **Above:** The DBX follows the trend of sporty SUVs in 2019.

The RB003 was content with a turbocharged V6 engine.

# THE MID-ENGINE BERLINETTAS

The most impressive display at the Geneva Car Show in 2019 was the one staged by Aston Martin. Its focus was on a proposed new line of mid-engine supercars in their various offshoots. The models in the range were cut from the same cloth; they shared the same architecture and had a common style. They were all developed under the direction of Fraser Dunn, the chief engineer in charge of advanced operations, in close cooperation with Red Bull Advanced Technologies. The work was led by the engineer Adrian Newey, who had created several Formula 1 championship-winning cars for Williams, McLaren and Red Bull. "Adrian took care of the invisible but crucial part for a grand touring machine, the surfaces under the car channelling the flows, while my team had to make the aerodynamic constraints aesthetically appealing; it was an exciting job!" says Marek Reichman animatedly. Under his authority, Miles Nurnberger, the director of design, sensitively created a common look; the respective functions of the cars were suggested by the subtle variations, some more gentle, some more aggressive.

Four different cars, but with similar silhouettes: a palette of futuristic saloons that would crown the Aston Martin range.

### From the RB001 (July 2016) to the Valkyrie (March 2017)

It all began in July 2016 at Silverstone on the fringes of the British Grand Prix with the unveiling of Project AM-RB001. Aston Martin didn't reveal any technical details at the time, but announced that this car would be part of a strictly limited series of 150. In March 2017, the RB100 was exhibited in Geneva under its true identity: Valkyrie. In January 2019, Aston Martin gave some supplementary details while insisting personalisation was possible through the 'Q by Aston Martin' programme, which allowed for a multitude of accessories, colours and materials. The Valkyrie might also benefit from the AMR Track Performance, designed to optimise the aerodynamic equipment, the running gear (magnesium rims), suspension and braking (titanium discs).

At the Geneva Car Show in 2019, it was established that Valkyrie would be fitted with a V12 at 65° produced by Cosworth, with a capacity of 6.5 litres, which would deliver 1,000 hp at 10,500 rpm and a torque of 740 Nm at 7,000 rpm.

An electric powertrain supplied by Rimac and Integral Powertrain Ltd would provide an additional 160 hp for a total of 1,160 hp at 10,500 rpm and 900 Nm of torque at 6,000 rpm.

In July 2019, a Valkyrie driven by Chris Goodwin would make its first public appearance at the opening event of the British Grand Prix.

### The Valkyrie AMR Pro (March 2018)

At the Geneva Car Show in 2018, the Valkyrie donned its sporting colours—a fluorescent yellow livery—in its AMR Pro version. It was a version reserved for circuits with a 'performance worthy of cars in the LMP1 category', said the manufacturer. A few figures were offered: the Valkyrie AMR Pro would be endowed with a hybrid engine totalling 1,100 hp. The production run would be limited to twenty-five.

### From Project 003 to the AM-RB003 (March 2019)

In March 2019, Project 003, quickly renamed the AM-RB003, presented in sky blue, was scheduled for a limited production of 500. This model would benefit from the lessons learned on the Valkyrie, but it would be less exclusive and equipped with a hybrid engine based on the V6 turbo.

### The Vanquish Vision Concept (March 2019)

Presented in dark green, this concept car is in the same spirit as the other mid-engined models. However, it was not built for the same purpose. Unlike the Valkyrie and the RB003, the Vanquish Vision Concept is housed in an aluminium chassis, not a carbon one. As it was not due to go on the market before 2022, the figures would be released later, but it was already known that the engine would come from the RB003 with an atmospheric V6.

Ugo Zagato, the first in a brilliant dynasty.

# DB + Z: A EULOGY TO EXCLUSIVITY

Unlike the various firms who took on the task of making special bodies for Aston Martin chassis, Zagato managed to build a real partnership.

The art of Italian bodywork had its golden age between the 1950s and the 1970s. Traditionally, these three decades have been defined in terms of the stimulating rivalry between Pinin Farina and Bertone. They represented two radically different attitudes to style, and defended their respective approaches with great panache. Between them they serviced most of the main constructors. However, as we saw with the genesis of the DB4 and DB5 lines, other creators—in this case Carrozzeria Touring—played a decisive role in the evolution of Aston Martin. Similarly, though in a more marginal way, the collaboration between Zagato and Aston Martin was crucial in reinforcing the British firm's elitist image.

Aston Martin used the 0177/R to promote its heritage.

# THE DB4 GT ZAGATO (1960–1962)

One year after the appearance of the DB4 GT, which would use a truncated form of the DB4 silhouette designed by Touring, Aston Martin unveiled a more spectacular variant which had its origins in the workshops of Zagato. Revealed at the London Motor Show in 1960, the DB4 GT is indisputably one of the most precious models in the whole history of Aston Martin. Zagato and his stylist Ercole Spada created a brand-new body on a short wheelbase. The sculptural harmony was not tarnished by gratuitous decoration. The traditional design of the grille was emphasised, and the volumes were handled in a way that accentuated the sportiness of the machine. The art of the bodywork builder resided here in the mastery of curves, in stark contrast with the stiffness of Touring.

The series consisted of nineteen cars distinguished from each other by unique artisanal touches: the contour of the grille, the air intakes on the bonnet, the pattern on the wings, the turn signals, the thickness of the wheel arches, the height of the passenger compartment.

# THE SPECIFICITY OF ZAGATO

Zagato occupies its own special place in the saga of Italian bodywork makers, if only because of the personality of its founder, who had learned about aviation technology during the First World War. Ugo Zagato was born on 25 June 1890 at Gavello in Venezia. After his military service, he got a job with the coachmaker Varesina.

In May 1915, Italy entered the war when it signed the London Pact to join the Triple Entente (France, Russia and Britain). Ugo Zagato then joined Fabbrica Aeroplani Ing. O. Pomilio. Without waiting for the end of hostilities, he founded Carrozzeria U. Zagato & C. in via Francesco Ferrer, Milan, in March 1919.

He was able to apply manufacturing techniques he had picked up in the aviation industry. Before becoming the maestro of sports bodywork, Zagato did work of a more conventional nature on some rather more prosaic vehicles.

It was in the sports field that Zagato expressed themselves most fully. In the course of the 1950s, several constructors came knocking on the door to ask them to make the most characteristic series in their catalogues: Fiat, Alfa Romeo, Lancia and Maserati. Aston Martin would join them in 1960.

0193/R with enlarged air outlet at the Rallye des Routes du Nord in 1964.

# THE DB4 GTS OF ZAGATO

**Top:** The DB4 GT Zagato no. 0176/R at Chantilly in 2014.
**Upper middle:** 0178/L entered in the Monaco Concours
d'Élégance in 2019. **Middle:** 0179/L at the 2013 Bensburg
Concours d'Élégance. **Lower middle:** 0180/L at the Chantilly
Concours d'Élégance in 2016. **Above:** 0181/L exiting the
Zagato workshops in 1961.

## 0176/R—July 1961

Beetroot-red bodywork; it was the car of the 1961 Geneva Motor
Show; for a long time the property of Hubert Fabri in France,
it was put up for sale by Gooding & Company in 2020.

## 0180/L—February 1961

White bodywork; sold to Jean Kerguen in Morocco, it
participated in the Le Mans 24 Hours in 1961; it was also
presented at the Chantilly Concours d'Élégance in 2016.

## 0177/R—December 1961

Originally metallic-blue bodywork; repainted in almond green,
it was used by Aston Martin communications.

## 0178/L—March 1961

Bright red body with enlarged rear wheel arches; sold new in
Switzerland, it participated in the Grand Prix de Spa in 1961 and
was presented by the Destriero collection at the 2019 Villa d'Este
Concours d'Élégance.

## 0179/L—February 1961

Silver-grey bodywork; sold new in Italy.

## 0181/L—March 1961

Almond-green bodywork with air intake on the hood; it was used
by Zagato for their communications, and was exhibited by Fisker
at Rétromobile in 2019.

### 0182/R—June 1961

Almond-green body with widened rear wings; registered 1 VEV for Essex Racing Stables, it participated in the Le Mans 24 Hours in 1961 and was presented at the Chantilly Concours d'Élégance in 2019.

### 0183/R—June 1961

Almond-green body with widened rear wings; registered 2 VEV for Essex Racing Stables, it participated in the Le Mans 24 Hours in 1961, then its front was modified in July 1962; it was sold for £10 million at Bonhams in 2018.

### 0187/R—October 1961

Blue body equipped with bumpers; it was exhibited at the Turin Car Show in 1961; repainted in almond green, it was entered in the Villa d'Este Concours d'Élégance in 2016 by an American collector.

### 0184/R—October 1961

Metallic-green bodywork; it was test driven in the magazine *Autocar* in April 1962.

### 0185/R—June 1962

Almond-green bodywork; it was presented by Blackhawk at Monterey in 2005.

### 0186/R—December 1961

White bodywork; it was sold new in Australia; repainted in metallic green, it reached a record high of $14.3 million in New York at RM Sotheby's in 2015.

### 0188/L—October 1961

Silver-grey bodywork (now navy blue) with headlights without profiling; it has long been part of the Blackhawk collection, which presented it at Pebble Beach in 2007.

**Top:** 0182/R at the weigh-in before the Le Mans 24 Hours in 1961. **Upper middle:** 0183/R victorious in the trial at the open GT race at Aintree in July 1961. **Middle:** 0187/R exhibited at the Turin Car Show with bumpers.
**Lower middle:** 0188/L is the only DB4 GT Zagato whose headlights are not profiled. **Above:** 0186/R presented at Villa d'Este in 2013.

**Top:** 0189/R presented at Villa d'Este in 2011.
**Upper middle:** 0190/L registered in Sweden visiting the Nürburgring in 1966. **Middle:** 0193/R before the start of the Le Mans 24 Hours in 1962. **Lower middle:** 0199/L fresh out of the Zagato workshops in Milan. **Above:** 0200/R and its distinctive decoration during its appearance at the 1960 London Motor Show.

### 0189/R—December 1962
Bluish-grey bodywork; it participated in the Villa d'Este Concours d'Élégance in 2011.

### 0199/L—December 1960
Metallic-green bodywork; repainted red when it was sold by RM in Monterey in 2005, then given a green livery in the Helena Collection for the Amelia Island 2015 Concours d'Élégance.

### 0190/L —June 1962
Silver-grey body with wide grid-style grille; it was exported to Sweden; in 2010, it was offered for sale by Kidston.

### 200/R—September 1960
Bodywork with chrome strip on the side; it was exhibited at the 1960 London Motor Show and participated in the 1962 Le Mans 24 Hours; it appeared at the Goodwood Revival in 2011 and 2012.

### 0191/R—June 1961
Grey body, low (type DP209); delivered new to John Coombs, she raced at Brands Hatch in May 1962.

### 0193/R—June 1962
Sky-blue body, low (type DP209); it was delivered in France to Jean Kerguen and took part in the Le Mans 24 Hours in 1962 and 1963.

In 1989, Aston Martin produced four replicas called 'Sanction II', which bore the numbers 0192/R, 0196/R, 0197/R and 0198/R. In 2019, Aston Martin added a DB4 GT Zagato Continuation to each of the nineteen DBS GT Zagatos.

# ERCOLE SPADA

Born in 1937, Ercole Spada belonged to the same generation as Marcello Gandini and Giorgetto Giugiaro. This Italian stylist built his reputation at Zagato, where he worked throughout the 1960s. His creations are strong and uncompromising. His name was attached to such memorable racing machines as the Aston Martin DB4 GT Zagato and the Alfa Romeo Giulia TZ.

Between 1976 and 1983, Ercole Spada was a close collaborator with Claus Luther at BMW in Munich. Among his designs are notably the 7 E32 Series and the 5 E34 Series. He returned to Zagato in September 1992. He left BMW to become head of design at LDEA, a design studio set up in Turin.

Aston Martin DB4 GTZ - 1960

**Top:** Ercole Spada is one of the major figures in the history of Zagato. **Above:** An original sketch by Ercole Spada for the DB4 GT Zagato.

# THE VANTAGE ZAGATOS (1986–1988)

As the V8, née DBS, reached the end of its life, Aston Martin and Zagato joined forces for one more showstopper. In March 1986, the Vantage Zagato was spectacularly launched: two cars were exhibited, one on the Aston Martin stand, the other on the Zagato stand, with a third fixed to the façade of the Hôtel Beau-Rivage, facing Lake Geneva. In Giuseppe Mittino's design, the V8 Vantage was unrecognisable with its taut lines and generous glass surfaces. The production run was limited to fifty, of which fourteen were left-hand drive.

In March 1987, a second series was launched, this time in the form of the Vantage Volante convertible. After the prototype (chassis no. 42), which was equipped with retractable headlights, the next thirty-six cars had the same front end as the coupé.

**Top:** As the Vantage V8 reached the end of its life, Zagato gave it an injection of modernity and Latin style. **Above:** The first of thirty-seven Vantage Volante models had retractable headlights.

Norihiko Harada dictated the Zagato style from the 1990s.

# THE SAGA OF THE LIMITED SERIES

Until the start of the new millennium, the constructors were happy to turn to independent designers and bodywork makers for a vision of the future, for reassurance or to pick up on new trends. This competition between in-house stylists and external studios fostered some healthy copying. Then, little by little, the manufacturers strengthened their own teams by making them more international, by employing designers from the increasingly sought-after design schools. In addition, the manufacturers transformed their processes. As their production lines became more and more flexible, they relied less and less on bodywork makers to make their marginal series. Faced with the gradual decline of their industrial activity, some bodybuilders reacted by reinventing themselves and returned to their core tradition, which consisted in creating one-off cars, designed to order, or coming up with strictly limited series for demanding (and affluent) customers who sought rarity and exclusivity.

This was the course chosen by Zagato, who attached the term 'workshop' to their name, evoking the original art of the panel-beater. The collaboration with Aston Martin resulted in several personalised series. In the first decade of the millennium. Zagato continued to cultivate the special relationship they had built up in the 1960s. Alongside the British firm's official catalogue, but with its approval, Zagato produced a number of limited series. In this period, the Zagato style was in the hands of Norihiko Harada, a Japanese designer born in November 1959 who had studied at Keio University in Tokyo.

## The DB7 Zagato (October 2002)

Appearing at the 2002 Paris Motor Show was this interpretation of the DB7, which, through its voluptuous volumes and sportiness, evokes the heritage of the DB4 GT Zagato. Ninety-nine would be produced in total.

## The DBAR1 (January 2003)

This roadster based on DB7 Zagato coupé was created for the American market. Unveiled at the Los Angeles Auto Show in January 2003, this American Roadster 1 was intended for drives on Highway One along the Pacific coast. A new series of ninety-nine was created.

Redesigned by Zagato, the DB7 was unrecognisable.

**Top:** The DBAR1 was tailor-made for Californian roads. **Above:** Created by Zagato, the 2004 Vanquish Roadster would be one of a kind.

## The Vanquish Roadster (March 2004)

When Aston Martin gave up on offering a Volante version of the Vanquish, Zagato took the matter in hand and tried to solve the delicate problem of the rigidity of the bodywork that arises on all convertibles.

Zagato's Vanquish Roadster adopted almost all the bodywork of the Vanquish Coupé; only the rear part was different, with a new shield and round red lights, common to many Zagato creations. Exhibited at the 2004 Geneva Car Show, this car would remain one of a kind.

# CENTENARIES

Age commands respect. All companies aspire to sustainability, durability and longevity. For this reason, they adore symbolic anniversaries. The two historic partners Aston Martin and Zagato would celebrate their centenaries just a few years apart, and these milestones would provide the pretext for some exceptional creations linking the two names.

The V12 Zagato on the track at the Nürburgring, driven by none other than Ulrich Bez, the boss of Aston Martin.

## THE V12 ZAGATO (MAY 2011)

Unveiled in a vermillion livery at the Concours d'Élégance in Villa d'Este, the V12 Zagato soon revealed its personality in a different décor: one week later, a second V12 Zagato—this one sporting a fluorescent green garb—competed in a trial of the VLN Championship at the Nürburgring circuit. So the V12 Zagato was a true racing car, based on the Vantage and supplied with the engine of the DB9. The style was the fruit of a close collaboration between Norihiko Harada at Zagato and Marek Reichman. Only sixty-five of the planned production run of 101 were actually produced.

The unique DB9 Centennial Spyder was sold for $693,000 by RM Sotheby's in Monterey in August 2015.

## The Centennials (2013–2014)

On the occasion of Aston Martin's centenary, Zagato paid homage to the brand with a novel and surprising design, quite at odds with their usual style. The profile traced by Norihiko Harada was atypical, with its long and straight belt line. The front end was just as unexpected, with the radiator grille occupying the entire surface. The same pattern would be rolled out in three distinct bodyworks, each with a different mechanical base.

The Centennial Coupé got things underway at Aston Martin's centenary celebrations in Kensington Gardens. The coupé, characterised by its double-bubble roof, was based on the DBS. It would turn up again on the stand of the magazine *Quattroruote* at the Geneva Car Show in 2014. The DB9 Centennial Spyder, which made its appearance alongside the DBS Centennial Coupé in Kensington, was conceived very much in the same spirit for the collector Peter Read, who passed on his treasure two years later.

Finally, a third variation on the Centennial theme—the shooting brake built on the mechanical base of the Virage—was paraded at the Concours Art and Élégance at Chantilly in September 2014.

Zagato's design for the Centennial was remarkable for the crispness of its lines.

# The Vanquish Zagato (2016–2017)

The collaboration between Aston Martin and Zagato produced a stunning new set of four models built on the mechanical base of the Vanquish. The more pronounced wings, the enlarged grille and the deeply sculpted flank reinforced the aggressiveness of the design.

- The Vanquish Zagato Coupé—the first of a series of ninety-nine—was presented at the Concours d'Élégance at Villa d'Este in May 2016. It satisfied the Zagato fetishists thanks to its double bubble roof, an idea often revisited by the company during the 1950s.

- The Vanquish Zagato Volante came out three months later at the Concours d'Élégance at Pebble Beach, again with a limited production of ninety-nine.

The Speedster version was the sportiest of the Vanquish Zagato range.

**Top left:** Very soon, the buyer of a Vanquish Zagato could choose the Volante convertible version: here being displayed at Chantilly in 2017. **Top right:** The first appearance of the Vanquish Zagato Coupé in the park at Villa d'Este in 2016. **Above:** With its Vanquish Zagato base, the shooting brake was closer to a coupé than an estate car.

- The Vanquish Speedster, more radical than the Volante, was distinguished by its two profiles that tapered behind the head rests; unveiled in August 2017, it was also the rarest of the quartet, with only twenty-eight produced,

- The Vanquish Zagato Shooting Brake came out at the same time as the Vanquish Zagato Speedster in 2017; with its receding, flattened rear end it was far removed from the original estate car. It too had a production run of ninety-nine.

**Top:** The sketch for the DB GT Zagato: a new myth. **Above:** The DBS GT Zagato was one of the most exclusive Aston Martins in history.

## The DBS GT Zagato (2019)

In October 2019, at Newport, Rhode Island, Aston Martin organised another marketing campaign that delighted collectors in search of exclusivity. This time, the DB4 GT Zagato Continuation and the DBS GT Zagato were presented in tandem—and put on sale likewise. The first was a perfect copy of the eponymous model from 1960, the second its modern transposition, The mechanical base of the DBS GT was that of the DBS Superleggera, with an extra shot of adrenaline provided by the twin-turbo V12 engine, souped up to 760 hp. Once again, the distribution of this sumptuous pair was fixed at the magic number of nineteen, a reference to the original DB4 GT Zagato. The price for the pair was £6 million; in terms of defending and illustrating their heritage: priceless.

# THE VANTAGE V12 ZAGATO
# HERITAGE TWINS (2019)

A long name for a bold and original concept: collectors were given the chance to acquire not just one exceptional car, but an inseparable duo consisting of a coupé and a speedster. The number of pairs was strictly limited to nineteen, the number of DB4 GT Zagatos that were produced. The coupé reprised the V12 Vantage Zagato of 2011, slightly updated, while the Speedster was brand new. Designed by Zagato, these cars were manufactured in R-Reforged's workshops in Warwick, UK. This company is part of the R-Universe group, which also owns R-Experience, R-Service and R-Motorsport, which is itself part of AF Racing based in Niederwil, Switzerland, the company responsible for developing the Aston Martins racing in championships open to the GT3 category. Connections everywhere.

**Top:** The V12 Zagato Heritage, coupé and speedster, only sold as a pair! **Bottom:** The DBS GT Zagato had to be bought with a modern reproduction of the DB4 GT Zagato. **Following pages:** The DBS GT Zagato used the mechanical base of the DBS Superleggera and honed it further.

# ASTON MARTIN STATISTICS: EVERY MODEL FROM 1940 TO 2021

## Private Cars

### ATOM (1940)
**Launched:** July 1940
**Engine:** 4 inline cylinders – OHC 1,950 cc (78 x 102 mm) then 1,970 cc (85 x 92 mm) – 90 hp at 5,000 rpm
**Chassis:** 259.1 x 157 x 157 cm
**Top speed:** 175 km/h
**Production:** 1 unit

### 2-LITRE SPORTS SPA SPECIAL (1948)
**Launched:** May 1948
**Engine:** 4 inline cylinders – OHV 1,970 cc (85 x 92 mm) – 100 hp at 4,750 rpm
**Chassis:** 274.3 x 137.2 x 137.2 cm
**Production:** 1 unit

### 2-LITRE SPORTS DROPHEAD COUPÉ (1948–1950)
**Launched:** London, October 1948
**Engine:** 4 inline cylinders – OHV 1,970 cc (85 x 92 mm) – 90 hp at 4,750 rpm
**Chassis:** 274.3 x 137.2 x 137.2 cm
**Dimensions:** 447 x 171.5 x 141 cm
**Production:** 14 units (including 1 bare chassis)

### DB2 (1950–1954)
**Launched:** New York, April 1950
**Engine:** 6 inline cylinders – DOHC 2,580 cc (78 x 90 mm) – 106 hp at 5,000 rpm (Vantage: 125 hp at 5,000 rpm)
**Chassis:** 251.5 x 137.2 x 137.2 cm
**Dimensions:** 430 x 165.1 x 135 cm
**Top speed:** 177 km/h (Vantage: 185 km/h)
**Evolution:** convertible in May 1950, Vantage option in January 1951, new front face April 1951
**Production:** 411 units (309 saloons + 102 DHCs)

### DB2-4 (1953–1955)
**Launched:** London, October 1953
**Engine:** 6 inline cylinders – DOHC 2,580 cc (78 x 90 mm) – 125 hp at 5,000 rpm
**Chassis:** 251.5 x 137.2 x 137.2 cm
**Dimensions:** 430.5 x 165.1 x 135.9 cm
**Top speed:** 190 km/h
**Evolution:** 2.9 litres 140 hp engine in April 1954
**Production:** 553 units (451 saloons + 102 DHCs)

### DB2-4 MARK II (1955–1957)
**Launched:** London, October 1955
**Engine:** 6 inline cylinders – DOHC 2,922 cc (83 x 90 mm) – 140 or 165 hp at 5,000 rpm
**Chassis:** 251.5 x 137.2 x 137.2 cm
**Dimensions:** 435.6 x 165.1 x 136 cm
**Top speed:** 193 km/h
**Evolution:** from April 1954, 2,922 cc (83 x 90mm) – 140 hp at 5,000 rpm
**Production:** 199 units (137 saloons + 34 FHCs + 24 DHCs + 4 chassis)

### DB MARK III (1957–1958)
**Launched:** March 1957
**Engine:** 6 inline cylinders – DOHC 2,922 cc (83 x 90 mm) – 162 hp at 5,500 rpm or 180 hp
**Chassis:** 251.5 x 137.2 x 137.2 cm
**Dimensions:** 435.6 x 165.1 x 136 cm
**Top speed:** 193 km/h
**Evolution:** 2.9 litre 140 hp engine from April 1954
**Production:** 651 units (462 saloons + 184 DHCs + 5 FHCs)

### DB4 (1958–1963)
**Launched:** Paris, October 1958
**Engine:** 6 inline cylinders – DOHC 3,670 cc (92 x 92 mm) – 243 hp at 5,500 rpm (Vantage: 266 hp at 5,750 rpm, Vantage GT: 302 hp at 6,000 rpm)
**Chassis:** 236.2 x 137.2 x 135.9 cm
**Dimensions:** 448 x 167.6 x 132.1 cm
**Top speed:** 225 km/h (Vantage: 230 km/h, Vantage GT: 245 km/h)
**Evolution:** Series II from February 1960, Series III in April 1961, Series IV in September 1961, Series V in September 1962, Vantage Option from September 1961. Convertible: Series I in October 1961, Series II in September 1962
**Production:** 920 units, including 840 coupés (150 S1s + 350 S2s + 64 S3s + 270 S5s + 6 Vantage GTs) and 80 convertibles (40 S1s + 40 S2s)

### DB4 GT (1959–1962)
**Launched:** Silverstone, May 1959
**Engine:** 6 inline cylinders – DOHC 3,670 cc (92 x 92 mm) – 306 hp at 6,000 rpm
**Chassis:** 236.2 x 137.2 x 135.9 cm
**Dimensions:** 435.3 x 167.6 x 132.1 cm
**Top speed:** 245 km/h
**Production:** 75 units

### DB4 GT ZAGATO (1960–1962)
**Launched:** London, October 1960
**Engine:** 6 inline cylinders – DOHC 3,670 cc (92 x 92 mm) – 318 hp at 6,600 rpm
**Chassis:** 236.2 x 137.2 x 136 cm
**Dimensions:** 435.3 x 167.6 x 132.1 cm
**Top speed:** 246 km/h
**Production:** 19 units (+ 4 Sanction IIs in 1989 + 19 Continuations in 2019)

### DB5 (1963–1965)
**Launched:** July 1963
**Engine:** 6 inline cylinders – DOHC 3,995 cc (96 x 92 mm) – 282 hp at 5,500 rpm (Vantage: 325 hp at 5,750 rpm)
**Chassis:** 248.9 x 137.2 x 135.9 cm
**Dimensions:** 457.2 x 167.6 x 134.6 cm
**Top speed:** 233 km/h (Vantage: 260 km/h)
**Evolution:** Vantage and shooting brake options in October 1964
**Production:** 1,158 units including 1,023 coupés (823 standard + 200 Vantage), 123 convertibles and 12 shooting brakes

The 2-litre Sports no. AMC/49/5 participating in the Le Mans 24 Hours in 1949.

## DB6 (1965–1969)

**Launched:** London, October 1965
**Engine:** 6 inline cylinders – DOHC
3,995 cc (96 x 92 mm) – 282 hp at 5,500 rpm
(Vantage: 325 hp at 5,750 rpm)
**Chassis:** 258.3 x 137.2 x 135.9 cm
**Dimensions:** 462.3 x 167.6 x 135.9 cm
**Top speed:** 238 km/h (Vantage: 245 km/h)
**Evolution:** Volante in October 1966 and Mark II in August 1969
**Production:** 1,753 units including 1,575 coupés (1,327 Mk Is + 248 Mk IIs) including 178 Volantes (140 Mk I + 38 Mk II) and 12 shooting brakes

## VOLANTE (1965)

**Launched:** July 1963
**Engine:** 6 inline cylinders – DOHC 3,995 cc (96 x 92 mm) – 282 hp at 5,500 rpm (Vantage: 325 hp at 5,750 rpm)
**Chassis:** 248.9 x 137.2 x 135.9 cm
**Dimensions:** 457.2 x 167.6 x 134.6 cm
**Top speed:** 230 km/h
**Production:** 37 units

## DBSC (1966)

**Launched:** Paris, October 1966
**Engine:** 6 inline cylinders – DOHC 3,995 cc (96 x 92 mm) – 325 hp at 5,750 rpm
**Chassis:** 258.5 x 137.2 x 135.9 cm
**Dimensions:** 444.5 x 168 x 123 cm
**Top speed:** 235 km/h
**Production:** 2 units

## DBS (1967–1972)

**Launched:** Paris, October 1967
**Engine:** 6 inline cylinders – DOHC 3,995 cc (96 x 92 mm) – 286 hp at 5,500 rpm (Vantage: 330 hp at 5,750 rpm)
**Chassis:** 261 x 149.8 x 149.8 cm
**Dimensions:** 458.5 x 182.9 x 132.7 cm
**Top speed:** 225 km/h (Vantage: 240 km/h)
**Production:** 787 units

## VANTAGE (1972–1973)

**Launched:** April 1972
**Engine:** 6 inline cylinders – DOHC 3,995 cc (96 x 92 mm) – 330 hp at 5,750 rpm
**Chassis:** 261 x 149.8 x 149.8 cm
**Dimensions:** 458.5 x 182.9 x 132.7 cm
**Top speed:** 240 km/h
**Production:** 70 units

## DBS V8 (1969–1972)

**Launched:** September 1969
**Engine:** 90° V8 – DOHC 5,341 cc (100 x 95 mm) – 381 hp at 5,500 rpm
**Wheelbase:** 261 x 149.8 x 149.8 cm
**Dimensions:** 458.4 cm, l: 182.9 cm, h: 132.7 cm
**Top speed:** 243 km/h
**Production:** 404 units

The V8 Volante Vantage brought the DBS line to a close.

### V8 (1972–1989)

**Launched:** September 1969 (V8 aka Series 2)
**Engine:** 90° V8 – DOHC 5,341 cc (100 x 95 mm) – 325–330 hp
   at 5,000 rpm
**Wheelbase:** 261 x 149.8 x 149.8 cm
**Dimensions:** 458.5 cm x 182.9 cm x 132.7 cm
**Top speed:** 240 km/h
**Evolution:** Series 3 in July 1973, Series 4 in October 1978 and
   Series 5 in January 1986
**Production:** 1,609 units (288 S2s + 967 S3s + 293 S4s + 61 S5s)

### V8 VANTAGE (1977–1989)

**Launched:** February 1977
**Engine:** 90° V8 – DOHC
5,341 cc (100 x 95 mm) – 375 hp at 6,000 rpm, then 403 hp at 6,250 rpm
**Chassis:** 261 x 150 x 150 cm
**Dimensions:** 466.7 x 189 x 132.7 cm
**Top speed:** 265 km/h
**Evolution:** Series 2 Oscar India in October 1978, X-Pack in October 1986
**Production:** 314 units (39 S1s + 138 S2s + 137 X-Packs)

### V8 VOLANTE (1978–1989)

**Launched:** June 1978
**Engine:** 90° V8 – DOHC 5,341 cc (100 x 95 mm) – approx. 315 hp
**Chassis:** 261 x 150 x 150 cm
**Dimensions:** 466.7 x 182.9 x 137 cm
**Top speed:** 210 km/h
**Evolution:** V8 Vantage Volante in October 1986
**Production:** 774 units (439 with carburettors + 168 with injection +
   167 Vantages)

### VANTAGE ZAGATO (1986–1988)

**Launched:** Geneva, March 1986
**Engine:** 90° V8 – DOHC 5,341 cc (100 x 95 mm) – 435 hp at
   6,000 rpm (Volante: 309 hp at 5,500 rpm)
**Wheelbase:** 261.1 x 152.7 x 154.4 cm
**Dimensions:** 438.9 x 185.9 x 130 cm (Volante: 448 x 186 x 130 cm)
**Top speed:** 298 km/h (Volante: 260 km/h)
**Evolution:** Volante version in March 1987
**Production:** 86 units (50 coupés + 37 Volantes)

### VIRAGE (1988–1995)

**Launched:** Birmingham, October 1988
**Engine:** 90° V8 – DOHC 5,341 cc (100 x 95 mm) – 330 hp at
   6,000 rpm
**Chassis:** 261.1 x 139.7 x 143 cm
**Dimensions:** 477 x 186.9 x 133.1 cm
**Top speed:** 250 km/h
**Evolution:** Volante version in September 1990, Limited Edition Coupé
   Engine 349 hp in October 1994
**Production:** 597 units (357 coupés + 7 Limited Edition Coupés +
   233 Volantes)

### VIRAGE 6.3 (1992–1996)

**Launched:** January 1992
**Engine:** 90° V8 – DOHC 6,347 cc (103.1 x 95 mm) – 465 hp at
   5,750 rpm, then 500 hp at 5,850 rpm
**Chassis:** 261.1 x 151 x 155 cm
**Dimensions:** 473.7 x 194.4 x 132.1 cm
**Top speed:** 280 km/h
**Evolution:** power increased to 500 hp in October 1993, twin-turbo
   version 550 hp in October 1992
**Production:** 24 units (21 coupés + 3 Volantes)

### V8 COUPÉ/V8 VOLANTE (1996–2000)

**Launched:** Geneva, March 1996
**Engine:** 90° V8 – DOHC 5,341 cc (100 x 95 mm) – 349 hp at
   6,000 rpm
**Chassis:** 261.1 x 151 x 152.2 cm (Volante LWB: 281 cm)
**Dimensions:** 474.5 x 191.8 x 133 cm
**Top speed:** 245 km/h
**Evolution:** Volante LWB in October 1997
**Production:** 164 units (101 coupés + 63 Volante LWBs)

### V8 VANTAGE (1992–1999)

**Launched:** Birmingham ; October 1992
**Engine:** 90° V8 – DOHC – twin-turbo 5,341 cc (100 x 95 mm) –
   550 hp at 6,500 rpm, then 600 hp
**Chassis:** 261.1 x 154.8 x 158.6 cm
**Dimensions:** 474 x 194 x 133 cm
**Top speed:** 300 km/h
**Evolution:** V600 version in 1996
**Production:** 248 units (239 coupés + 9 Volante SWBs)

### V8 VANTAGE LE MANS (1999–2000)
**Launched:** Geneva, March 1999
**Engine:** 90° V8 – DOHC – twin-turbo 5,341 cc (100 x 95 mm) – 550 or 600 hp at 6,500 rpm
**Chassis:** 261.1 x 154 x 158 cm
**Dimensions:** 474.5 x 194.4 x 133 cm
**Top speed:** 320/330 km/h
**Production:** 40 units

### DB7 (1993–1999)
**Launched:** Geneva, March 1993
**Engine:** 6 inline cylinders – DOHC – turbo 3,228 cc (91 x 83 mm) – 335 hp at 5,500 rpm
**Chassis:** 259.1 x 151.6 x 153.1 cm
**Dimensions:** 464.6 x 183 x 123.8 cm
**Top speed:** 266 km/h
**Production:** 2,457 units (1,578 coupés + 879 Volantes)

### DB7 VANTAGE (1999–2003)
**Launched:** Geneva, March 1999
**Engine:** 60° V12 – DOHC 5,935 cc (89 x 79.5 mm) – 420 hp at 6,000 rpm
**Chassis:** 259.1 x 151.6 x 153.1 cm
**Dimensions:** 469.2 x 183 x 124.3 cm
**Top speed:** 295 km/h
**Production:** 4,150 units (2,091 coupés + 2,059 Volantes)

### DB7 GT (2002–2003)
**Launched:** Birmingham, October 2002
**Engine:** 60° V12 – DOHC 5,935 cc (89 x 79.5 mm) – 435 hp at 6,000 rpm
**Chassis:** 259.1 x 151.6 x 153.1 cm
**Dimensions:** 469.2 x 183 x 124.3 cm
**Top speed:** 298 km/h
**Production:** 303 units (191 GTs + 112 GTAs)

### DB7 ZAGATO (2002)
**Launched:** Paris, October 2002
**Engine:** 60° V12 – DOHC 5,935 cc (89 x 79.5 mm) – 440 hp at 6,000 rpm
**Chassis:** 259.1 x 151.6 x 153.1 cm
**Dimensions:** 448.1 x 186.2 x 124.5 cm **Top speed:** 300 km/h
**Production:** 99 units

### DBAR1
**Launched:** Paris, October 2002
**Engine:** 60° V12 – DOHC 5,935 cc (89 x 79.5 mm) – 440 hp at 6,000 rpm
**Chassis:** 259.1 x 151.6 x 153.1 cm
**Dimensions:** 466 x 186 x 124 cm
**Top speed:** 300 km/h
**Production:** 99 units

### DB9 (2003–2016)
**Launched:** Frankfurt, September 2003
**Engine:** 60° V12 – DOHC 5,935 cc (89 x 79.5 mm) – 450 hp at 5,750 rpm, then 470 hp at 6,000 rpm, then 517 hp at 6,500 rpm
**Chassis:** 274 x 156.8 x 156.2 cm
**Dimensions:** 470.9 x 187.5 x 131.8 cm
**Top speed:** 295–307 km/h
**Evolution:** Volante in January 2004, second series with 470 hp engine in July 2008, third series with 517 hp engine in October 2012
**Production:** more than 16,500 units of all versions of the DB9

### DB9 GT (2015–2016)
**Launched:** Goodwood, June 2015
**Engine:** 60° V12 – DOHC 5,935 cc (89 x 79.5 mm) – 547 hp at 6,750 rpm
**Chassis:** 274 x 156.8 x 156.2 cm
**Dimensions:** 472 x 206.1 x 128.2 cm
**Top speed:** 295 km/h
**Production:** n.a.

### DB9 CENTENNIAL SPYDER (2013)
**Launched:** London, July 2013
**Engine:** 60° V12 – DOHC 5,935 cc (89 x 79.5 mm) – 517 hp
**Chassis:** 274 x 156.8 x 156.2 cm
**Dimensions:** n.a.
**Top speed:** 300 km/h
**Production:** 1 unit

### VIRAGE (2011–2012)
**Launched:** Geneva, March 2011
**Engine:** 60° V12 – DOHC 5,935 cc (89 x 79.5 mm) – 497 hp at 6,500 rpm
**Chassis:** 274 x 158.5 x 158 cm
**Dimensions:** 470.3 x 190.4 x 128.2 cm
**Top speed:** 300 km/h
**Production:** approx. 1,000 units

### VIRAGE CENTENNIAL SHOOTING BRAKE (2014)
**Launched:** Chantilly, September 2014
**Engine:** 60° V12 – DOHC 5,935 cc (89 x 79.5 mm) – 497 hp at 6,500 rpm
**Chassis:** 274 x 158.5 x 158 cm
**Dimensions:** n.a.
**Top speed:** 300 km/h
**Production:** 1 unit

### DB10 (2014–2015)
**Launched:** London, December 2014
**Engine:** 90° V8 – DOHC 4,735 cc (91 x 91 mm) – 436 hp at 7,000 rpm
**Chassis:** 270.5 x 157 x 156 cm
**Dimensions:** 440 x 220.4 x 125 cm
**Top speed:** 310 km/h
**Production:** 10 units

### DB11
**Launched:** Geneva, March 2016
**Engine:** 60° V12 – DOHC 5,204 cc (89 x 69.7 mm) – 608 hp at 6,500 rpm
**Chassis:** 280.5 x 165.7 x 162.4 cm
**Dimensions:** 473.9 x 206 x 127.9 cm
**Top speed:** 322 km/h
**Evolution:** in July 2017 variant with V8 twin-turbo engine (4.0 litres 510 hp)
**Production:** ongoing

### VANQUISH (2001–2004)
**Launched:** Geneva, March 2001
**Engine:** 60° V12 – DOHC 5,935 cc (89 x 79.5 mm) – 460 hp at 6,800 rpm
**Chassis:** 269 x 155 x 157 cm
**Dimensions:** 466.5 x 192.3 x 131.8 cm
**Top speed:** 306 km/h
**Production:** 1,503 units

## VANQUISH ROADSTER (2004)
**Launched:** Geneva, March 2004
**Engine:** 60° V12 – DOHC 5,935 cc (89 x 79.5 mm) – 460 hp at 6,500 rpm
**Chassis:** 269 x 155 x 157 cm
**Dimensions:** n.a.
**Top speed:** 305 km/h
**Production:** 1 unit

## VANQUISH S (2004–2007)
**Launched:** October 2004
**Engine:** 60° V12 – DOHC 5,935 cc (89 x 79.5 mm) – 520 hp at 7,000 rpm
**Chassis:** 269 x 155 x 157 cm
**Dimensions:** 466.5 x 192.3 x 131.8 cm
**Top speed:** 322 km/h
**Production:** 1,086 units

## DBS (2007–2012)
**Launched:** Pebble Beach, August 2007
**Engine:** 60° V12 – DOHC 5,935 cc (89 x 79.5 mm) – 510 hp at 6,500 rpm
**Chassis:** 274 x 157 x 156 cm
**Dimensions:** 472.1 x 190.5 x 128 cm
**Top speed:** 307 km/h
**Evolution:** Volante version in March 2009
**Production:** 3,379 units (2,533 coupés + 846 Volantes)

## DBS CENTENNIAL COUPÉ (2013)
**Launched:** London, July 2013
**Engine:** 60° V12 – DOHC 5,935 cc (89 x 79.5 mm) – 510 hp at 6,500 rpm
**Chassis:** 274 x 157 x 156 cm
**Dimensions:** n.a.
**Top speed:** 300 km/h
**Production:** 1 unit

## VANQUISH (2012–2016)
**Launched:** Cernobbio, May 2012
**Engine:** 60° V12 – DOHC 5,935 cc (89 x 79.5 mm) – 573 hp at 6,750 rpm
**Chassis:** 274 x 158.5 x 158 cm
**Dimensions:** 472 x 191 x 129.4 cm
**Top speed:** 295 km/h
**Evolution:** Volante version in June 2013
**Production:** n.a

## VANQUISH S (2016–2018)
**Launched:** Los Angeles, November 2016
**Engine:** 60° V12 – DOHC 5, 935 cc (89 x 79.5 mm) – 603 hp at 7,000 rpm
**Chassis:** 274 x 159 x 159 cm
**Dimensions:** 466.5 x 192.3 x 131.8 cm
**Top speed:** 322 km/h
**Evolution:** Volante version in March 2017
**Production:** n.a.

## VANQUISH ZAGATO (2016–2018)
**Launched:** Cernobbio, May 2016
**Engine:** 60° V12 – DOHC 5,935 cc (89 x 79.5 mm) – 595 hp at 7,000 rpm
**Chassis:** 274 x 159 x 159 cm
**Dimensions:** 473 x 191 x 129.5 cm
**Top speed:** 320 km/h
**Evolution:** Volante version in August 2016, shooting brake and speedster in August 2017
**Production:** 325 units (including 99 coupés, 99 Volantes, 99 shooting brakes and 28 speedsters)

## DBS SUPERLEGGERA (2018–)
**Launched:** London, June 2018
**Engine:** 60° V12 – DOHC 5,204 cc (89 x 69.7 mm) – 715 hp at 6,500 rpm
**Chassis:** 280.5 x 166.5 x 164.5 cm
**Dimensions:** 471.2 x 214.6 x 128 cm
**Top speed:** 340 km/h
**Evolution:** Volante version in April 2019
**Production:** ongoing

## DBS GT ZAGATO (2019–2020)
**Launched:** Newport, October 2019
**Engine:** 60° V12 – DOHC 5,204 cc (89 x 69.7 mm) – 760 hp
**Chassis:** 280.5 x 166.5 x 164.5 cm
**Dimensions:** 471.2 x 214.6 x 128 cm
**Top speed:** 340 km/h
**Production:** 19 units

## ONE-77 (2009–2012)
**Launched:** Cernobbio, April 2009
**Engine:** 60° V12 – DOHC 7,312 cc (94 x 87.8 mm) – 760 hp at 6,500 rpm
**Chassis:** 279.1 x 170.6 x 170.6 cm
**Dimensions:** 460.1 x 220.4 x 122.2 cm
**Top speed:** 350 km/h
**Production:** 77 units

## VULCAN (2015–2016)
**Launched:** Geneva, March 2015
**Engine:** 60° V12 – DOHC 6,949 cc – 820 hp at 7,750 rpm
**Chassis:** n.a.
**Dimensions:** 480.7 x 206.3 x 125.5 cm
**Top speed:** 355 km/h
**Production:** 24 units

## DBX (2019–)
**Launched:** Los Angeles, November 2019
**Engine:** 90° V8 – twin-turbo – DOHC 3,982 cc (83 x 92 mm) – 550 hp at 6,500 rpm
**Wheelbase:** 306 cm
**Dimensions:** 503.9 x 205/222

The DBR1 Thea dominated the 1959 endurance season.

## Racing Cars

### DB3 (1951–1952)

**Launched:** September 1951

**Engine:** 6 inline cylinders – DOHC 2,580 cc (78 x 90 mm) 140 hp at 5,000 rpm

**Chassis:** 236.2 x 129.5 x 129.5 cm

**Dimensions:** 402.6 x 156.2 x 101.6 cm

**Top speed:** 254 km/h

**Evolution:** from 1952 2.9 litre engine (78 x 90 mm), 163 hp at 6,000 rpm

**Production:** 9 units (4 factory spiders + 3 spiders for clients + 2 coupés for clients)

### DB3 S (1953–1955)

**Launched:** May 1953

**Engine:** 6 inline cylinders – DOHC 2,922 cc (83, x 90 mm) 182, then 225 hp at 6,000 rpm

**Chassis:** 221 x 124.4 x 124.4 cm

**Dimensions:** 390.7 x 149.4 x 104 cm

**Top speed:** 230–240 km/h

**Evolution:** dual-ignition engine in 1954

**Production:** 30 units (8 factory spiders + 2 factory coupés + 17 spiders for clients + 3 coupés for clients)

### DBR1 (1956–1960)

**Launched:** Le Mans, June 1956

**Engine:** 6 inline cylinders – DOHC 2,922 cc (83 x 90 mm) – 240–254 hp at 6,250 rpm

**Chassis:** 228.6 x 130.8 x 130.8 cm

**Dimensions:** 402.6 x 162.6 x 97.8 cm

**Top speed:** 250 km/h

**Evolution:** DBR1-300 variant from August 1957

**Production:** 5 units (4 factory + 1 private)

### DBR2 (1957)

**Launched:** Le Mans, June 1957

**Engine:** 6 inline cylinders – DOHC 3,910 cc (95 x 92 mm) – 298 hp at 5,700 rpm

**Chassis:** 236.2 x 134.6 x 134.6 cm

**Top speed:** 270 km/h

**Production:** 2 units

### DBR4 (1959)

**Launched:** Silverstone, May 1959

**Engine:** 6 inline cylinders – 2 act – 2,493 cc (83 x 76.8 mm) – 280 hp at 7,800 rpm

**Chassis:** 236.2 x 130.8 x 130.8 cm

**Top speed:** 260 km/h

**Production:** 4 units

### DP212/DP215 (1962–1963)

**Launched:** Le Mans, June 1962

**Engine:** 6 inline cylinders – DOHC 3,996 cc (96 x 92 mm) – 335 hp at 6,000 rpm

**Chassis:** 238.8 x 137.2 x 137.2 cm

**Dimensions:** 442 x 167.6 x 127 cm

**Top speed:** 300 km/h

**Evolution:** DP215 in 1963

**Production:** 2 units (1 DP212 + 1 DP215)

### DP214 (1964)

**Launched:** Le Mans, April 1964

**Engine:** 6 inline cylinders – DOHC 3,749 cc (93 x 92 mm) – 314 hp at 6,000 rpm

**Chassis:** 238.8 x 139.7 x 136.2 cm

**Dimensions:** 442 x 167.6 x 121.9 cm

**Top speed:** 290 km/h

**Production:** 2 units

### AMR1 (1989)

**Launched:** Silverstone, November 1988

**Engine:** 90° V8 – DOHC 6,300 cc – 700 hp at 8,000 rpm

**Chassis:** 289.6 x 160 x 152.4 cm

**Dimensions:** 477.5 x 198.1 x 101.6 cm

**Top speed:** 350 km/h

**Production:** 5 units

The following models and their derivatives fell outside the criteria for this book: V8 Vantage, V12 Vantage, Cygnet and Valkyrie.

# ACKNOWLEDGEMENTS

## A Big Thank You

This book was based on numerous reports I have made at Aston Martin Lagonda over the past decades. I was able to find out about new models and then meet with the company's leaders thanks to the cooperation of Bettina Walhart, who has long been responsible for communication of the brand in France along with Alain Aziza, the head of Aston Martin Paris, the brand's official, authorised dealer.

I would like to thank Bettina very much for allowing me throughout these years to discover and experience the inexpressible charms of Aston Martin cars.

My gratitude is extended also to Judith Richter, Head of Public Relations at Aston Martin in Frankfurt. She provided liaison between continental Europe ... and the factory, now in a country far away from Europe!

Of course, throughout the realisation of this book, Sophie Lecompte was, as usual, my invaluable contact at Glénat, skilfully coordinating the writing, the artwork and the artistic direction.

My warmest thanks to all of them.

Serge Bellu

## Photography Credits

**Inside pages: Archives Grand Tourisme:** 10, 13 (t), (b), 14, 18, 20 (b), 24 (um), (lm), (b), 28 (t), (m), (b), 29 (t), (um), (lm), (b), 30, 31, 32, 34, 35 (l), (r), 36, 37 (tl), (tr), (b), 38, 39 (l), (r), 40, 41 (t), (b), 44, 45 (t), (b), 46 (t), (b), 47, 48, 49 (t), (b), 50 (tl), 51, 54 (b), 56, 57, 58 (t), (b), 61 (l), (r), 63, 65, 68, 69 (tl), (m), (tr), (bl), (br), 72 (t), (b), 73, 74 (t), (b), 76-77, 78, 79 (b), 80, 82, 83, 86 (tl), (tr), 88 (tl), 98, 103 (ml), (mr), 109, 114, 122, 123, 124 (t), 127, 129, 132, 135, 141 (t), 144, 153, 154 (b), 155 (t), (um), (m), (lm), 156 (um), (m), (lm), (b), 157 (b), 158 (b), 161 (t), 171; **Aston Martin Lagonda:** 7, 9, 12, 16, 19, 22, 24 (t), 42, 50 (tr), 62, 64-65, 66, 90, 110, 124 (b), 125, 126, 128 (tl), (tr), (b), 130, 133 (t), (b), 134, 136, 137 (r), 138 (t), (b), 139, 140, 141 (b), 142-143, 145 (t), (b), 146 (t), (bl), br), 147 (t), (b), 148, 152, 158 (t), 161 (b), 162, 164, 165 (b), 166 (t), (b), 167 (t), (b), 168-169, 175; **Aston Martin Lagonda/Archives Grand Tourisme:** 3, 84, 86 (b), 87, 91 (b), 92 (t), 93, 94 (b), 95, 96, 101, 102, 103 (b), (t), 104, 105, 106-107, 108, 112, 113 (t), (b), 115, 116, 117, 118 (tl), (tr), (ml), (mr), (b), 119, 120-121; **Bellu:** 154 (t), (um), (m), 155 (b), 156 (t), 157 (t), 165 (tr); **Bonhams:** 15 (tl), 20 (t), 21, 26, 27 (b), 50 (b), 54 (t), 70 (t), (b), 79 (t), 81, 92 (b), 94 (t), 172; **DR:** 27 (t), 52-53, 75, 88 (tr), 89 (b), 99; **Gooding & Company:** 23; **Jaguar:** 100; **Peter & associés:** 154 (lm), 165 (tl); **Red Bull Racing:** 137 (l); **RM Auction:** 91 (t); **RM Sotheby's:** 15 (tr), 15 (b), 25, 33, 55, 59, 60, 71, 89 (t), 163 (t); **Zagato:** 150, 159, 160, 163 (b).

Abbreviations: left (l), right (r), top (t); bottom (b); middle (m); top left (tl); top right (tr), bottom left (bl), bottom right (br), middle left (ml), middle right (mr), top centre middle (tcm), upper middle (um), lower middle (lm)